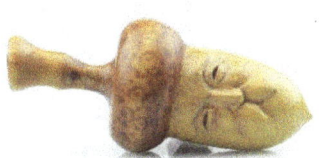

Fantasy Acorn
Wood
Circa 1990
John L. Heatwole III
Father of the Author

Do It Dave's

Anyone Can Draw: Trees

Workbook #1 Gridding

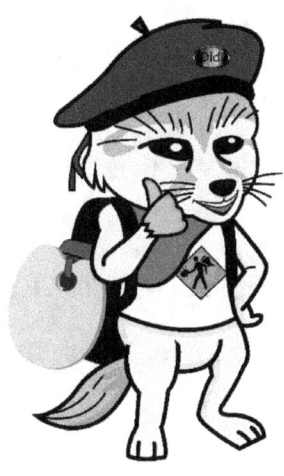

Copywrite © 2021 David F. Heatwole All rights reserved.

Do It Dave's Anyone Can Draw: Trees
Workbook #1 Gridding

ISBN: 978-1-7374110-0-0

No part of this publication may be reproduced, distributed, or transmitted in any form or by any means, including photocopying, recording, or electronic or mechanical methods, without the prior written permission of the publisher, except in the case of brief quotations embodies in reviews and certain other non-commercial uses permitted by copyright law.

The information provided herein is meant to help individuals of all ages and all walks of life learn to see the world around them. Neither the author nor publisher makes any promises to magically create master artisans who will make a fortune with their art or even, for that matter, make a dollar. However, if one can pick up a pencil and render whatever they see, they may just be able to convince another to buy him or her a cup of coffee or a loaf of bread – but no promises there either.

Learn more about the artist at www.ThisArtistsDream.com

Published by The Art Studios of David F. Heatwole, LLC

49 Jacqueline Drive, Berea, Ohio 44017

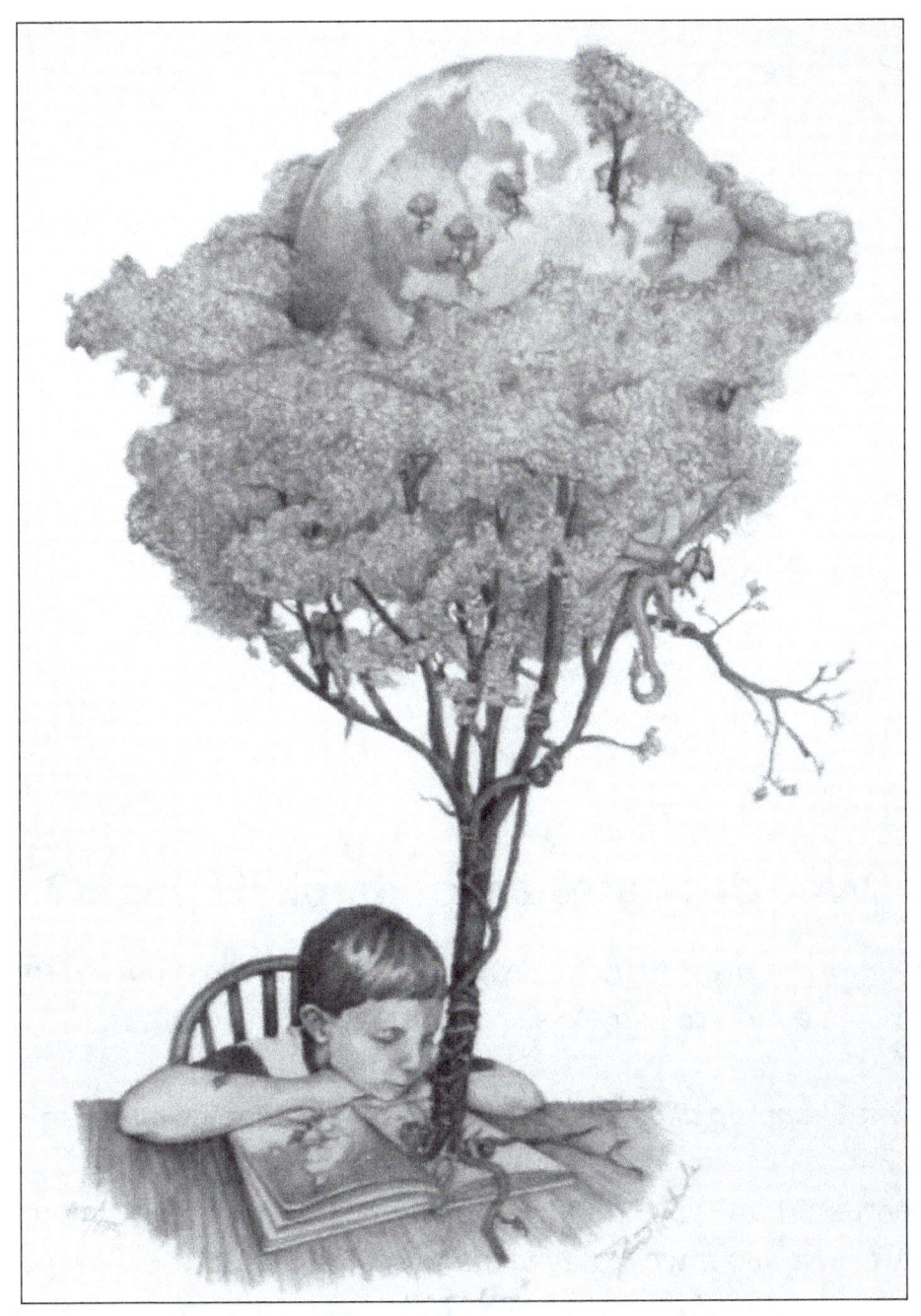

"Environmental Fiction" by David F. Heatwole
circa 1990, Graphite on paper

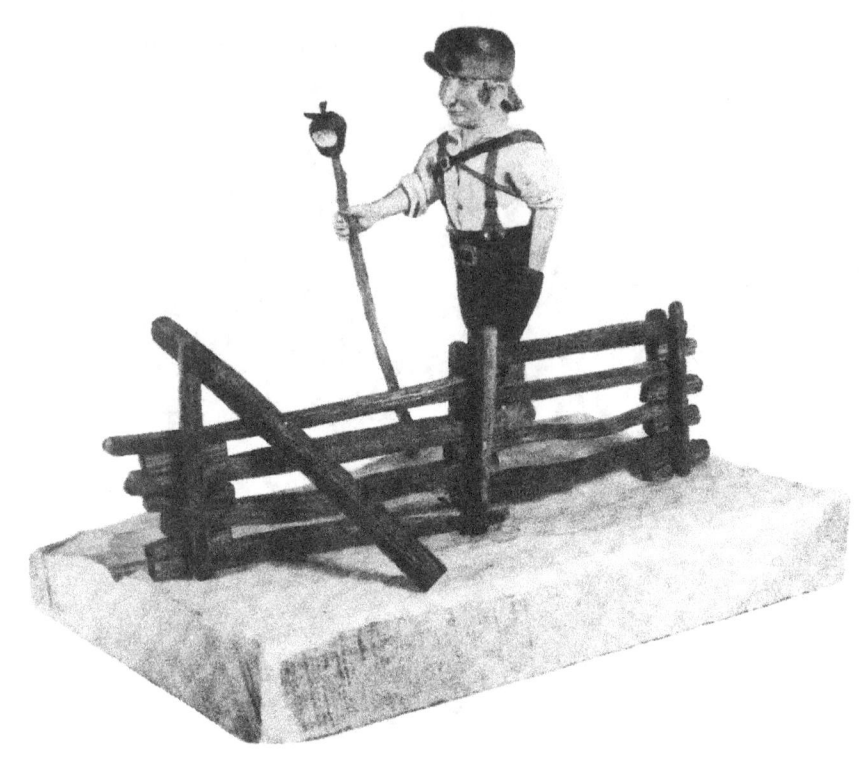

Johnny Appleseed
Wood
Circa 1975
John L. Heatwole III

Who dedicates a workbook?!? Right?

In memory of my father, The Wizard of Wood, who modeled for me a magical way to see things. I will never forget.

To John Chapman aka. Johnny Appleseed for planting all those trees!

LASTLY, a long overdue "Thank you" to Buck Brown. A 7th grade classmate who taught me how to draw a tree in Art class and it wasn't even our assignment. Buck Brown you might never see this dedication, but I will never forget you doing this. I even remember the table where we were sitting.

This drawing workbook, the first in my series, is primarily meant to be for the beginning practitioner of the visual arts. Like all workbooks from this series, I share tools, tricks, and skills that I have learned throughout my 40+ years in the arts. Regardless of your age, the principles I teach herein have been used for countless generations by well-established fine art painters and the students who trained to be so.

In this first of my workbooks for aspiring artists the student will work hard learning how to use a grid to copy and transfer an image to another surface.

So, what is a grid? The simplest grid is a system of intersecting lines that create square or rectangular cells. A small grid would be an arrangement of four cells, two on top and two on the bottom (see EXHIBIT A). An infinite number can be used to build a grid of intersecting lines, resulting in infinite cells. It depends on the space in which to build this framework that will limit its size. If it is an 8.5" x 8.5" square piece of paper, then the grid, regardless of how many lines you use, will limit the amount of information you can place on it.

The idea of using a grid to learn how to draw a picture is basically a way to break an image, regardless of how simple or

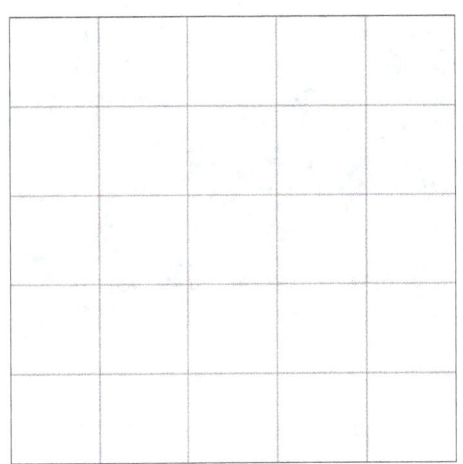

Exhibit A: a 5 by 5 grid makes 25 squares.

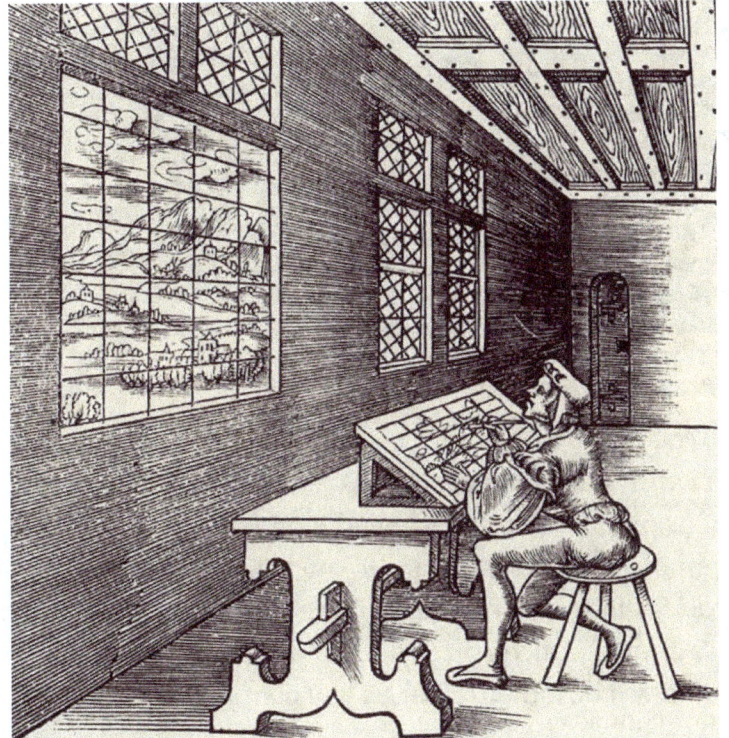

Hieronymus Rodler's version of Alberti's Veil (1531).

complex it is, into bite-sized pieces by overlaying a grid onto the drawing, photo, or living subject matter I will explain this last example in greater detail further in this document.

As I mentioned, by drawing a grid or overlaying a grid on top of an image, you can see inside each cell only a certain amount of information, whether it be lines or shapes; from now on, let's call this gridded; subject: **"gridded subject."** On a blank piece of paper, you have another grid drawn out on the material you want to transfer the image onto; from now on, let's call this the **"grid surface."**

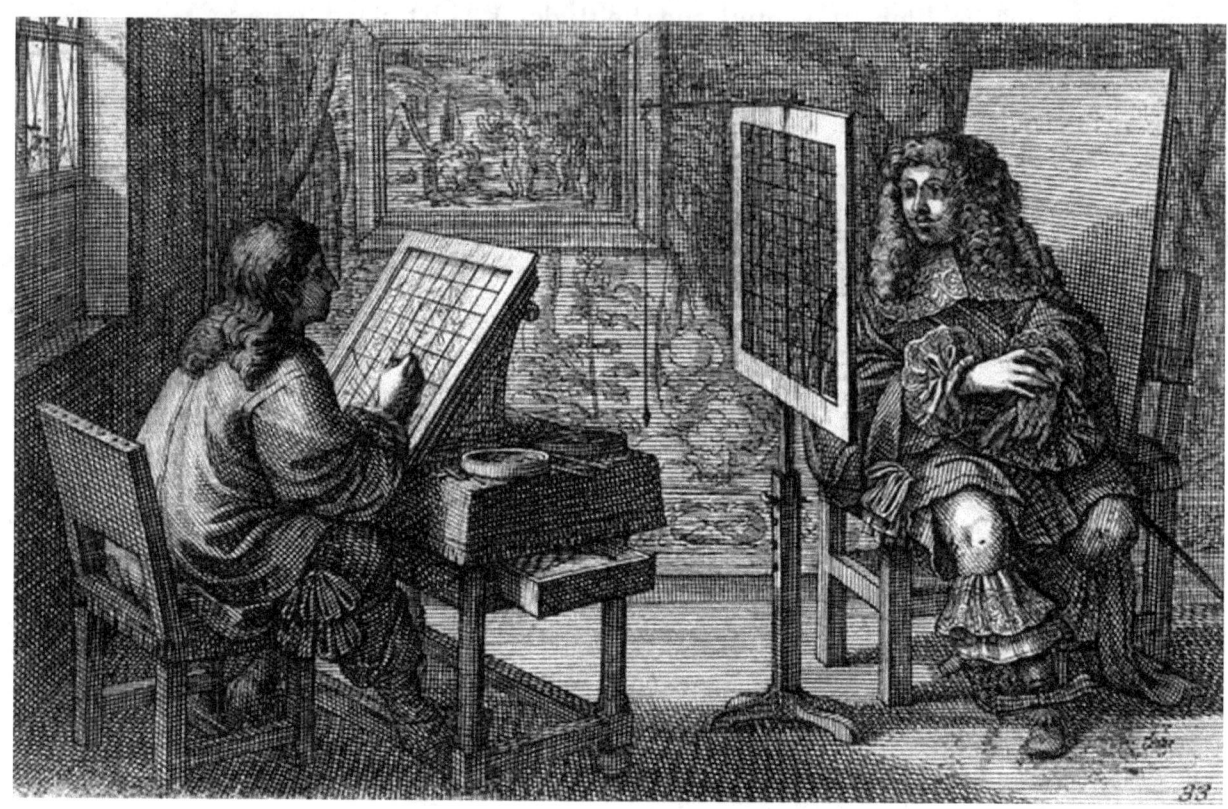

Abraham Bosse, a portrait artist using a grid (1737).

However, understand that the substrate or material you want to transfer the image to can be any type of material, shape, or size. With this workbook, we work with paper known as a two-dimensional surface; with that in mind, we are also mainly discussing other 2-dimensional surfaces like canvas, wood, a brick wall (although it has three-dimensional surfaces). Still, this grid system can also be used for 3-dimensional objects. A typical example of what I mean is transferring an image to a round globe that has been primed white and then drawing a grid onto it. Drawing the grid will not be easy, but it is doable. Once you understand the principle of the grid, you can take it as far as you like. The principles of the grid will become clearer as you continue with the various exercises herein.

Okay, so the grid cell you are looking at on the gridded subject must correspond with the same grid cell on the grid surface. See examples on the next page. However, your grid on the gridded subject might only have quarter-inch square cells, while the grid cells on the grid surface might be one-foot square. In our case, the square format for the cells allows you, the artist, to see easily the detail found in each of the cells on your gridded subject and scale it up appropriately. Grids, however, do not need to be square formats; they can be rectangular. They can alternatively be made out of triangles or octagons. The amount of work required to draw those out would be very time-consuming and, in my opinion, not worth the effort. You can purchase papers and pads of paper that already have grids printed on them, but their size restrictions may limit you. Check online or at your local art and office supply stores. Online you should be able also to find printable graph paper. Your best bet, though, is to draw it yourself.

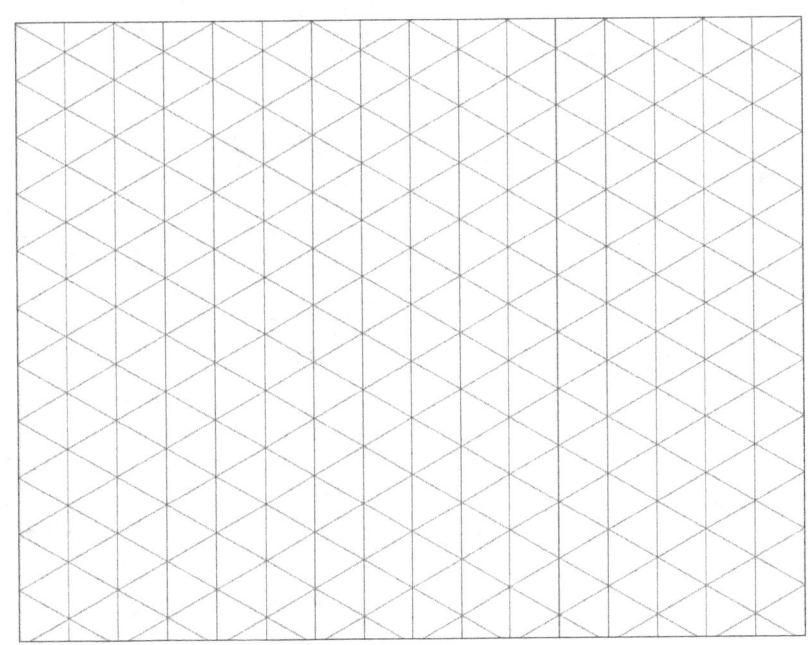

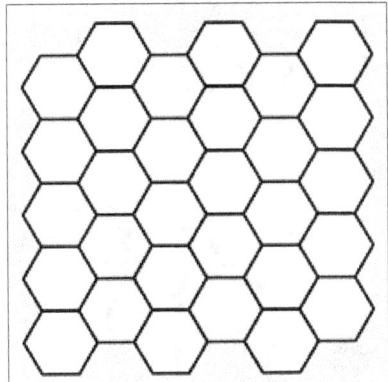

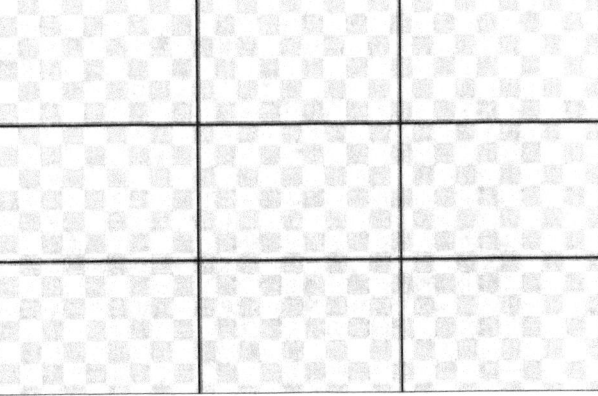

Here are some examples of different grids than what we are working with in this workbook. The above grid is clearly made to show triangles but there are so many more shapes that can be found just by staring at it. The grid on the far left is made of hexagon shapes. Can you see hexagons in the triangle grid above? The last grid to the left shows a rectangular 3 by 3 grid and is the closest to the square grid we will be working with.

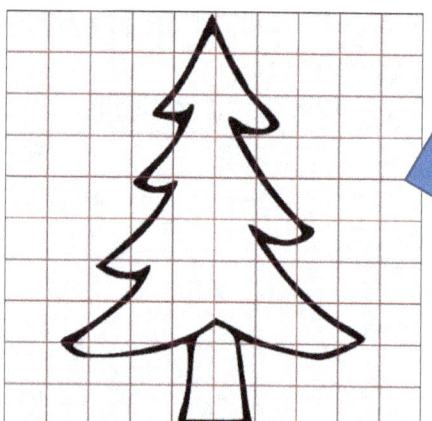

Above is a clip art image of a pine tree that is approximately two inch square. By placing a 10 by 10 grid over the drawing and creating another grid where the 10 x 10 grid is actually 30 feet by 30 feet it will be easy to enlarge the image to paint a mural as close to the small original as possible without using a projector and tracing the image.

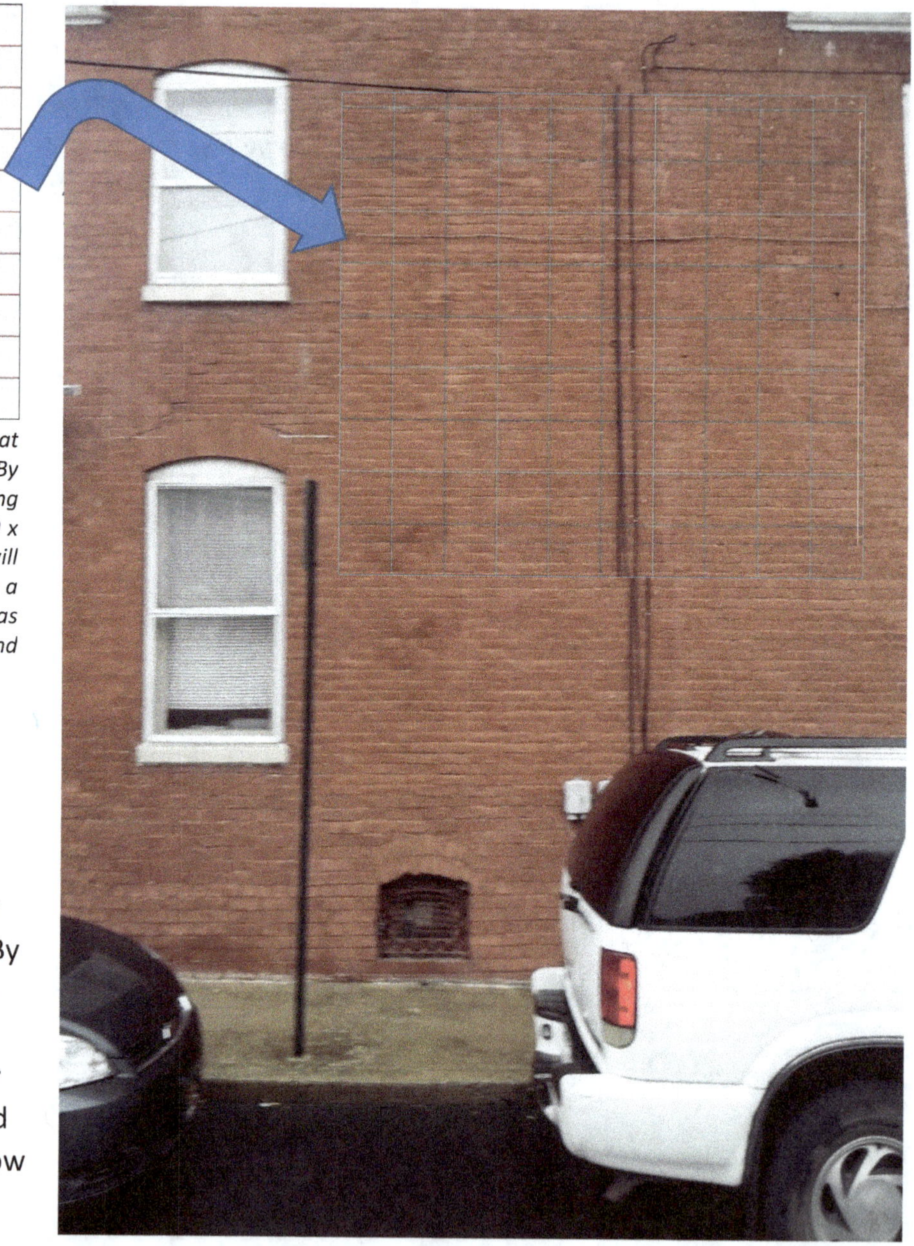

When muralists want to make a replica of a drawing or painting created on a much smaller scale, they may use a grid system to transfer and enlarge their image to the wall. By overlaying a grid on the image to be transferred that will correspond with a larger grid marked off on another surface, an image can be enlarged almost precisely depending on how much detail they want to put into it.

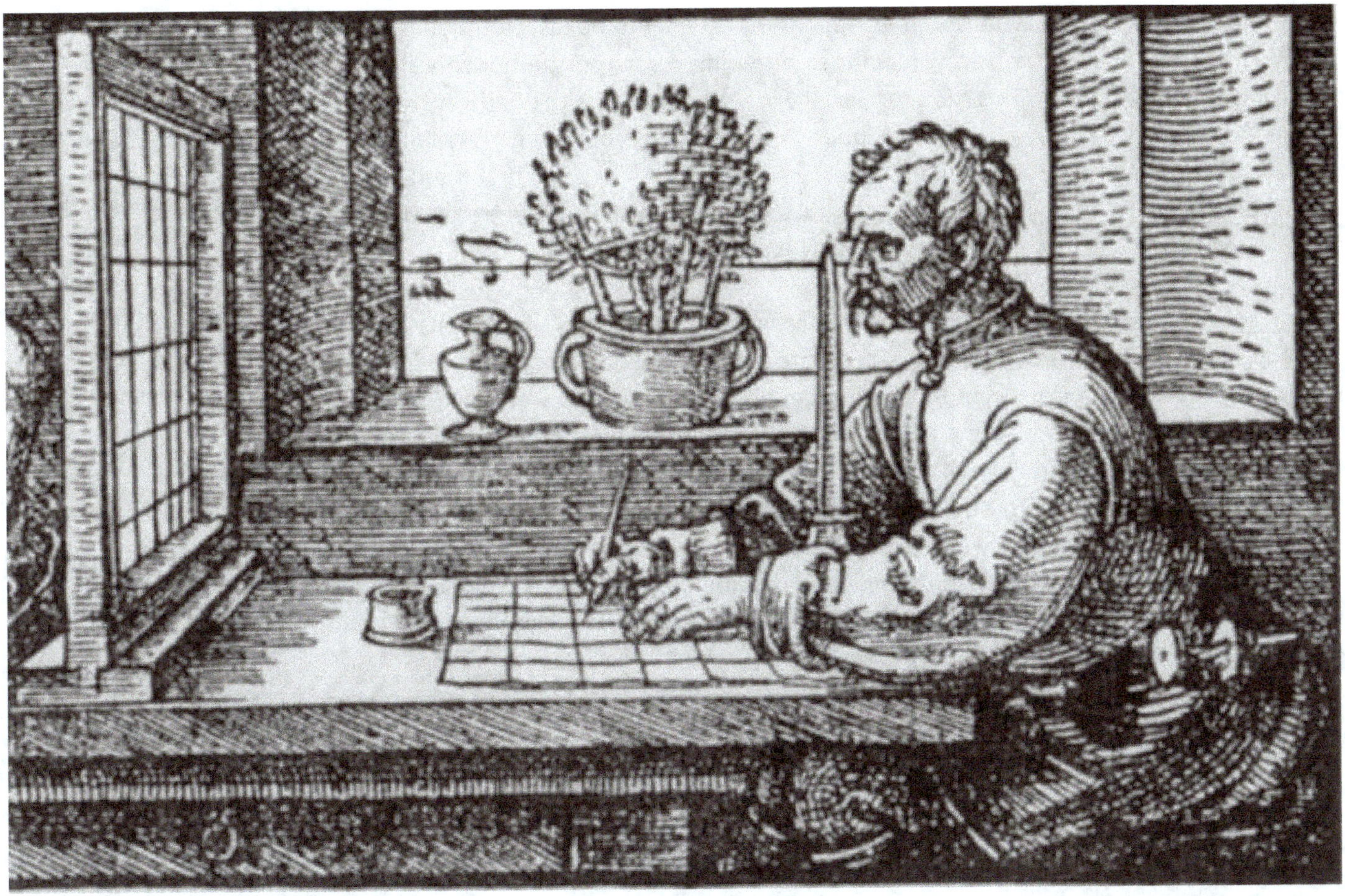

Figure 1: The illustration above by Albrecht Durer shows how an early artist might have used a grid device, called a "Sighting Grid", to help them capture a subject. The grid lines divided the subject, allowing the artist to draw on their paper, marked with a grid, the exact location of each objects, allowing the artist to basically trace what they could see with their eyes.

If you look through the workbook, you will see that each tree illustration and each exercise with more grid cells, or less in some cases, will get more complicated and may seem tedious at first. This workbook is designed with a lot of thought to help you get to a point where you should be able to observe and draw what you look at better than ever before.

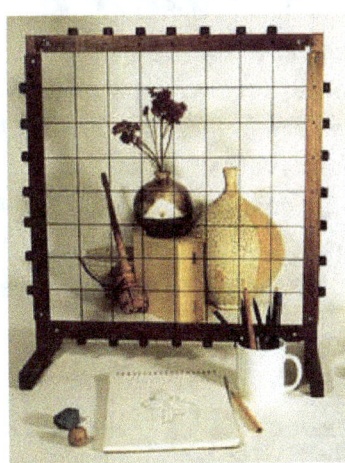

Figure 2: A still life with the "Sighting Grid" a contraption that would allow the artist to collect information from each cell of the grid allowing the individual to transfer the information to their substrate of choice. In the photo it is a pad of paper.

The following six pages show a simple outline of a pine tree. This drawing has been set into grids so you can see details as they appear in certain grid boxes. Your job is to identify where the line of the tree you want to draw intersects on the horizontal or vertical lines of the grid box. This requires visually identifying where the halfway mark of a line is or what a quarter of a line. It requires seeing where your image is falling in the space of a grid cell because, in many cases, your subject matter will first intersect a grid line but will continue into gridline the grid's cell. This will also require dividing your box up visually using the x and y-axis, much like reading a map.

Illustration 1

X and Y axis of a grid Before directional services such as Garmin, MapQuest, and Google Maps, to name a few, that tells you where to go and even where not to go if there is an accident. People used paper maps to get around places they were unfamiliar with. These maps used a grid with an X-axis and a Y-axis. The X-axis is the numerically labeled vertical grid lines traveling across the page from left to right. The Y Axis is the series of alphabetically labeled horizontal lines crossing across the page from one side of the paper to the other. To locate a place on the map, you would first look up the name of the place in the index (see Figure 1). The index would have the town's name with a corresponding location afterward made up of numbers and letters. The numbers can be found on the top and bottom of the vertical grid lines, and the letters are on the sides of the horizontal map grid lines. Let's say you are looking up my childhood town of Bridgewater in the Virginia Map; in the index, it would read Bridgewater 66 A4. The number 66 first indicates the page to turn to; the A would indicate the alphabetically labeled horizontal line drawn across the page. With your eyes or figure on the horizontal line A, you would move to the right until you land on the 4th vertical line labeled as such on the top of the page. Where these two lines meet is the approximate location of the town. (See Figures 2 and 3 for the map example)

Bretton Woods 58 C1
Briarwood 34 B3
Bridgeport 56 C2
Bridges 50 B2
Bridgetown 51 A5
Bridgewater 66 A4
Bridle Creek 23 D7
Briery 46 D1

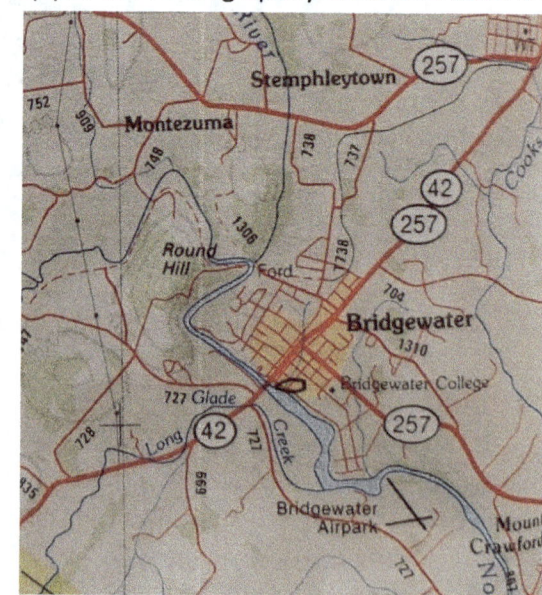

Figure 2: portion of an index from a DeLORME Virginia Atlas & Gazetteer - Topography map.

Figure 2: detail of Topography map shows the town of Bridgewater, Virginia.

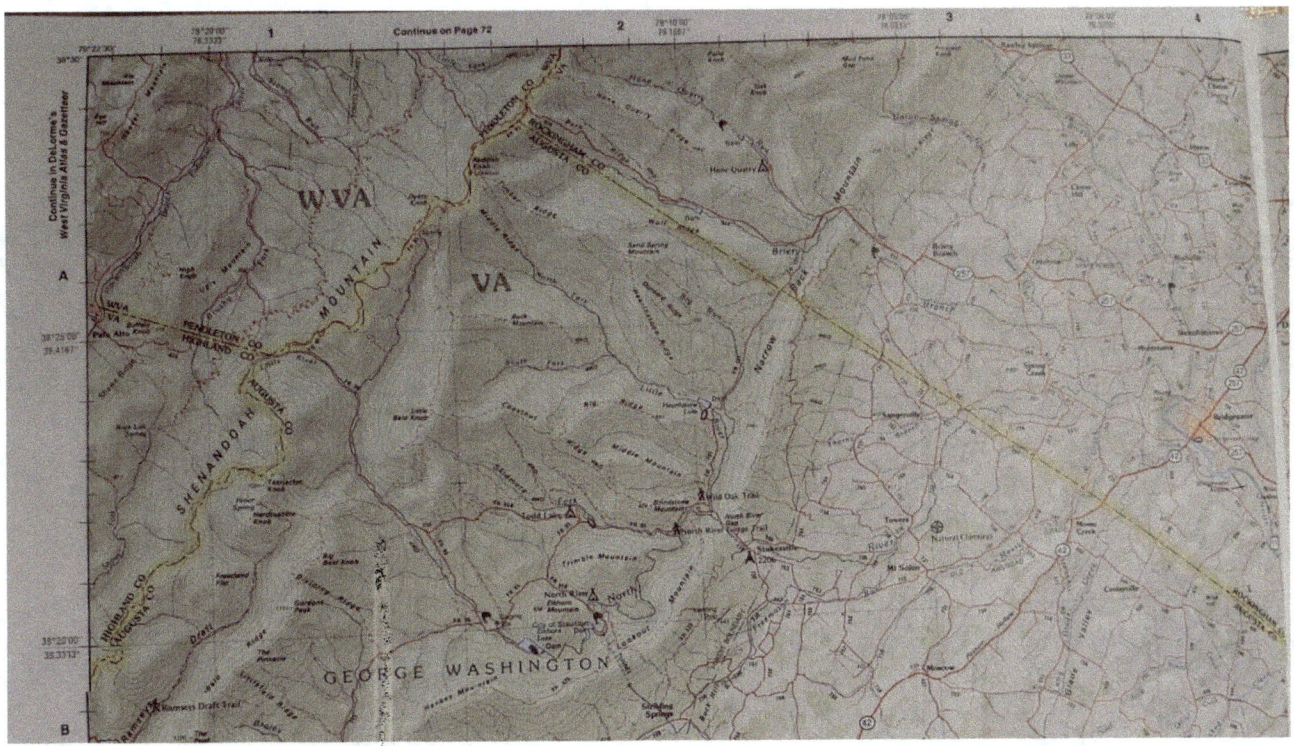

Figure 3: Topography map of parts of Virginia and West Virginia. There are faint lines leading across the page where the letter A and B are seen on the left border of the page and line traveling down the page at each of the numbers seen at the top of the map.

THE ART OF OBSERVATION

Much like using a map of X and Y coordinates, you can see in Illustration 2 that the top of the pine tree seen in Illustration 1 is intersecting walls of four quadrants. The first thing to note is that this line is not simply a pencil or pen line but instead has a body and shapes shaped in different sections. Therefore, it is crucial to understand that you aren't dealing with one line but two to draw this tree. These lines are invisible and are only for you to see. What you are drawing is the outline of two shapes, the shape of the negative space, in this case, all the white area, and the positive space, which would be the black form. Once you start to look at the shapes, you will discover the

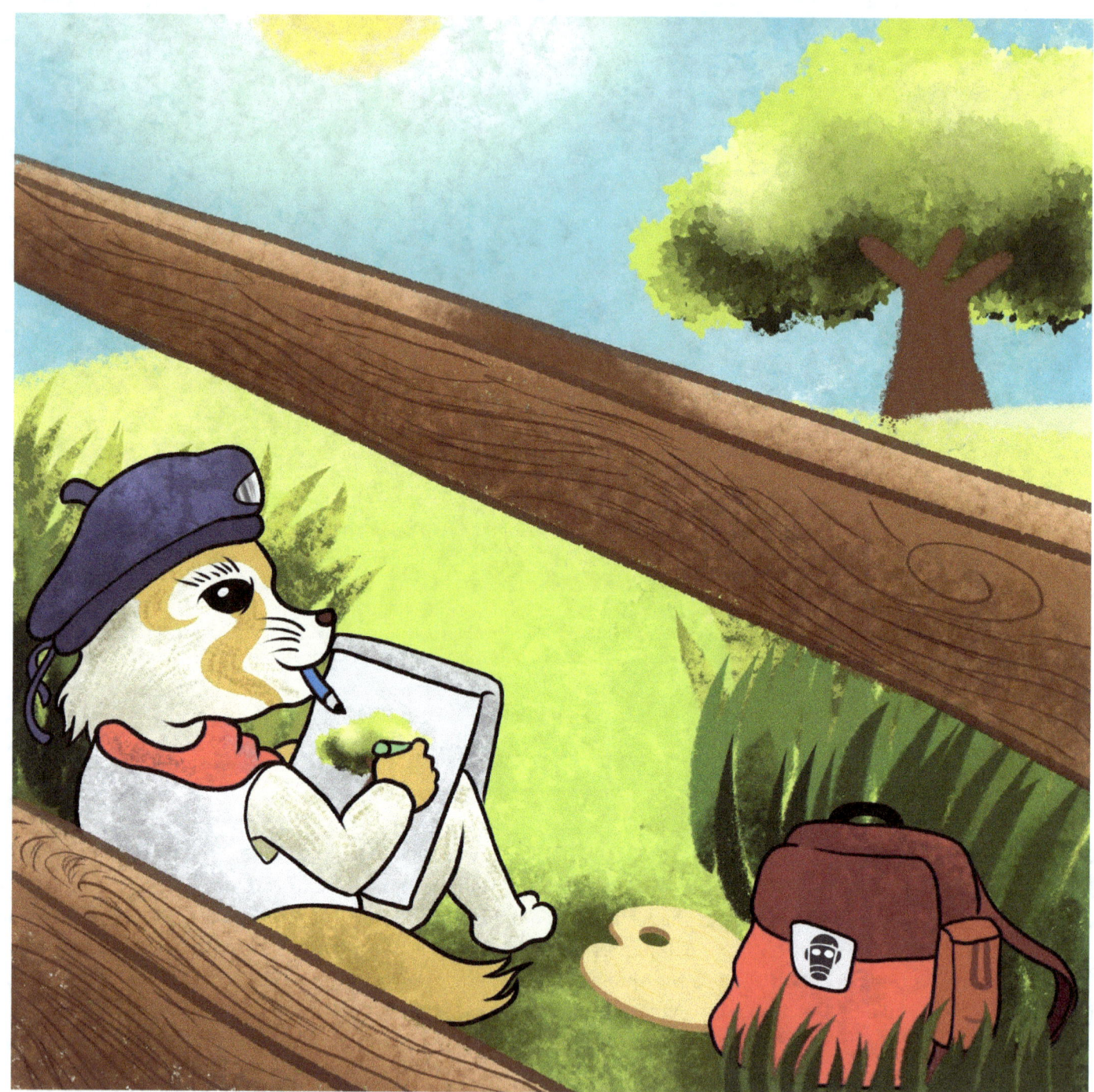

Figure 4 Illustration by wowyellowstudio in cooperation with David F. Heatwole, 2021

lines you need to draw. Once those lines are drawn, then you would color in the black form. Let's start in cell 3. The line comes up from the bottom of the cell just inside the right of the center point of the bottom line. The line curves slightly upward to the right side of the cell and lands almost precisely in the center of the vertical right line, where it intersects and moves into quadrant four. It then goes a fourth of the way into cell 4 where it stops shy of the top of the cell and then goes back down and then to the left, crossing the line between the two cells back into cell 3 again about a quarter of the way into the cell before it takes a sharp turn upward toward cell 2. Notice that the line is not straight; it bows in a little toward the center of the tree.

This exercise is about observing lines, shapes, curves, and intersections. It requires visually dissecting lines and measuring. If you need to start with a tape measure, go for it, but in my opinion, it is better just to do it. You may notice as you get going that your eyes are constantly darting from one shape to another, one line to another, as you are visually measuring and comparing locations of where lines meet. In Illustration B below you can see the detail of cell #2 in Illustration A. I have divided this detailed cell even further to illustrate how you need to mentally divide up a grid cell while discerning where the information is in relation to the outside cell walls. Mentally splitting the cell into mid-points so that when you are about to transfer the information in the cell on the gridded subject to the grid surface, you can do so with great precision. In this illustration, I have divided the cell up into a 6 by 6 grid.

Illustration A

Illustration B

The first thing we need to establish is that this thick line of the tree is not just a thin pencil line. The outline of the tree has a thickness to it. This is super important because the line is thicker in some areas, and you would want to transfer as much of this information to your grid surface as possible. Here is a great example: In Illustration B, I have zoomed in on the cell numbered 2 from Illustration A and have divided this cell even more with lines that are only to explain what you need to be looking for. Do you see that the top of the tree does not land directly in the center of the top line of the grid cell? It falls just inside to the left of the halfway mark. Now look below the sharp point of the tree. The underneath part of the thick line is rounded and does not come to a point. The curved part lands between the first and second division lines. Now, look at the top of the tree line; it goes from the top to the bottom right corner of the cell. It also does not intersect with the corner. It intersects with the bottom cell line just shy of the corner. Remember, the thickness of the lines makes a total of six or more lines that you have to consider and draw out just in this one cell. Like with anything, the more you practice, the better you will get. DON'T LET THE GRID IN ILLUSTRATION C INTIMIDATE YOU; IT IS ONLY FOR INFORMATIONAL PURPOSES AND IS REALLY ONLY A MENTAL GRID. It will help if you are contineously comparing and dividing spaces, asking yourself where things are in relation to other things nearby, intersecting, overlapping, or simply sitting in a space.

In Illustration C below, I have, for simplicity's sake, kept the top of the tree with a grid just to show you how the points discussed earlier actually are mentally recognized while trying to transfer the image. Notice all the red dots? Those are all the points where the line crosses the horizontal and vertical grid lines. The two purple dots are not intersecting the grid lines but indicate specific details you need to pay special attention to because they are essential to the design. In this case, the purple dots indicate where one must start to curve a line. See Illustration C for a detail of this area.

Illustration D shows two purple lines that indicate where the shape of the tree is starting to get larger and then curve.

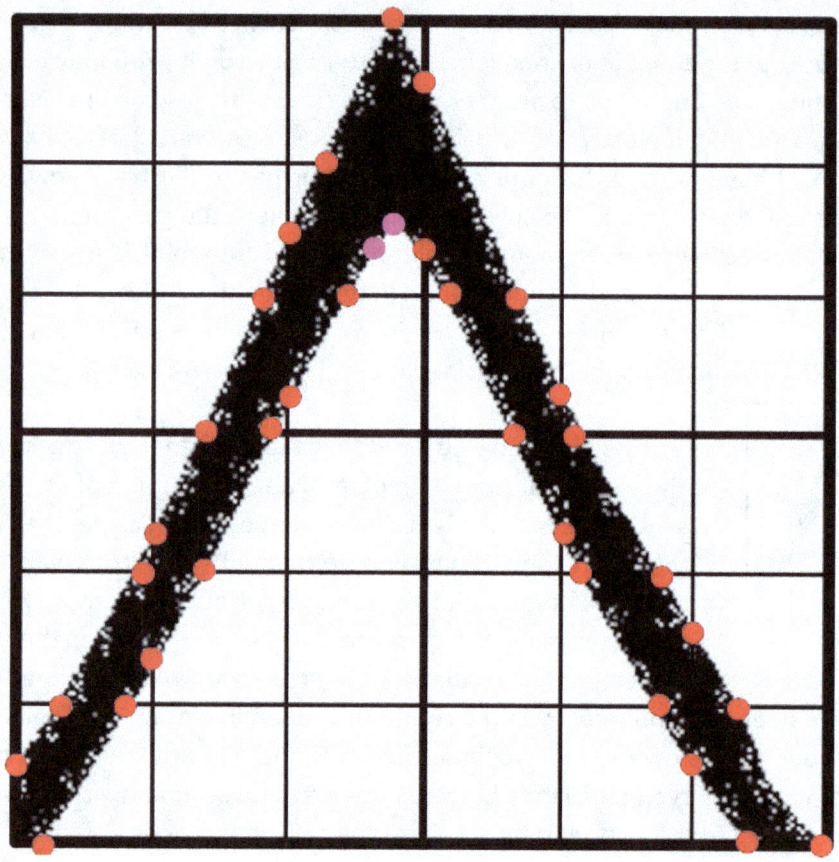

Illustration C

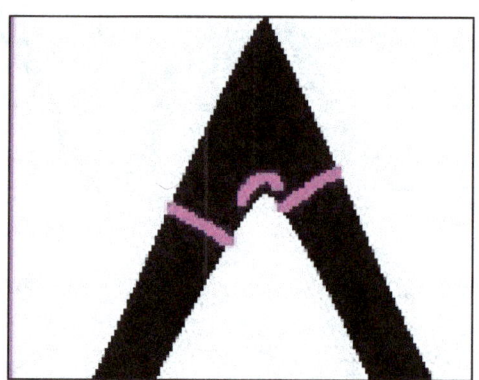

Illustration D

HERE WE GO!

ARE YOU READY TO BEGIN?

The following pages are workbook pages for you to try transferring the image of the pine tree on a 1 to 1 basis, but throughout this exercise will get more complex and get you to a point where you could enlarge an image.

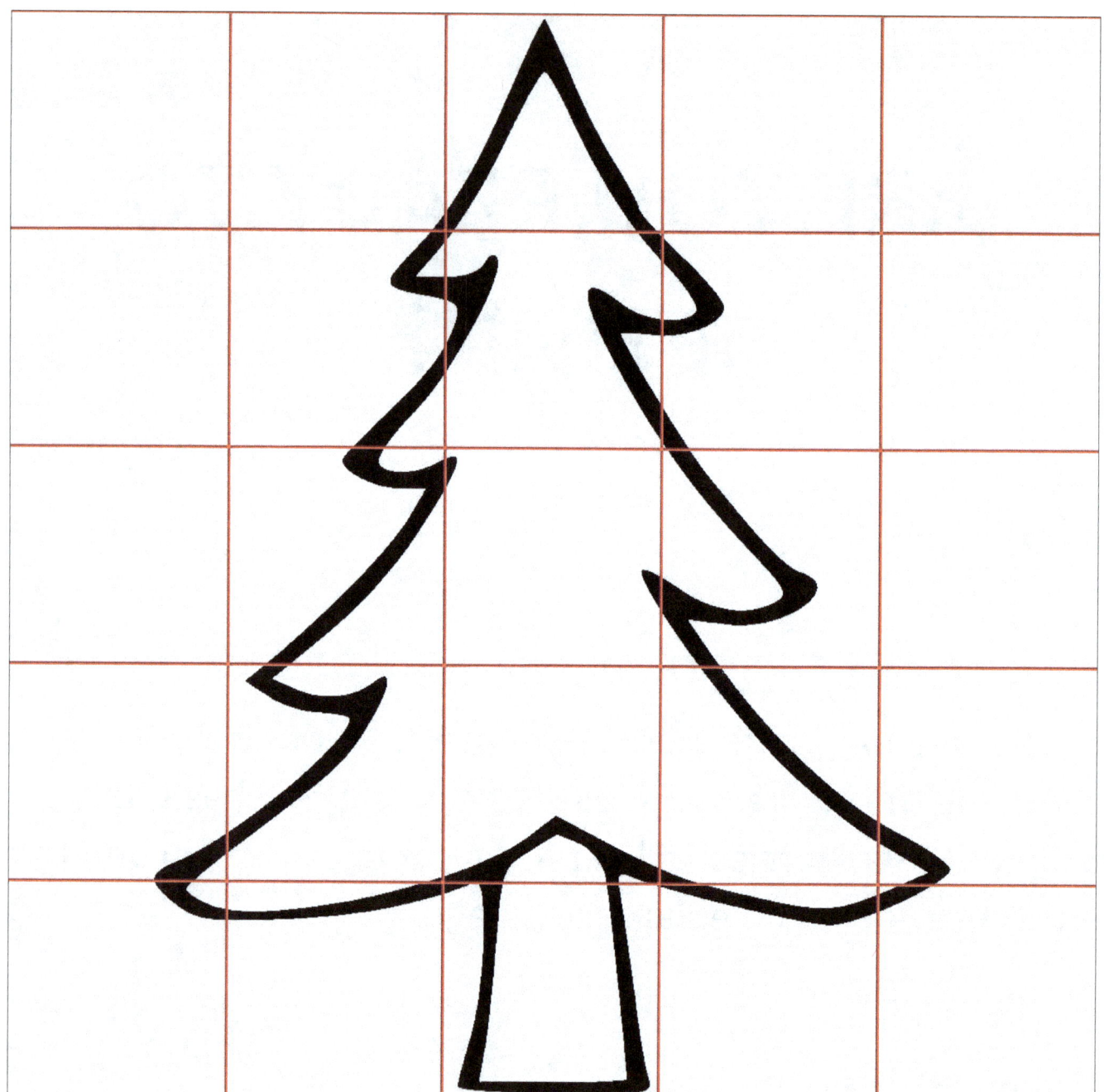

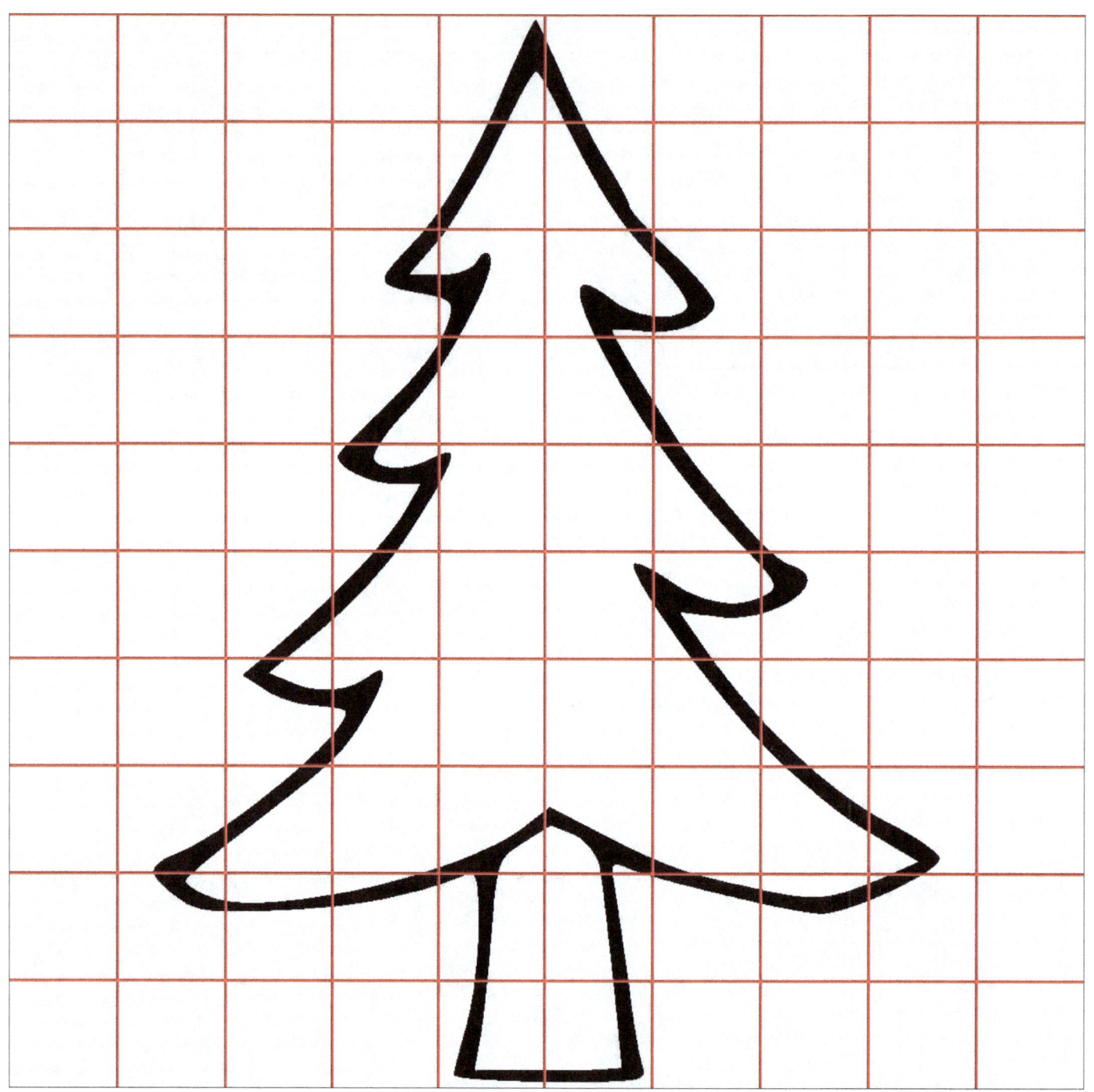

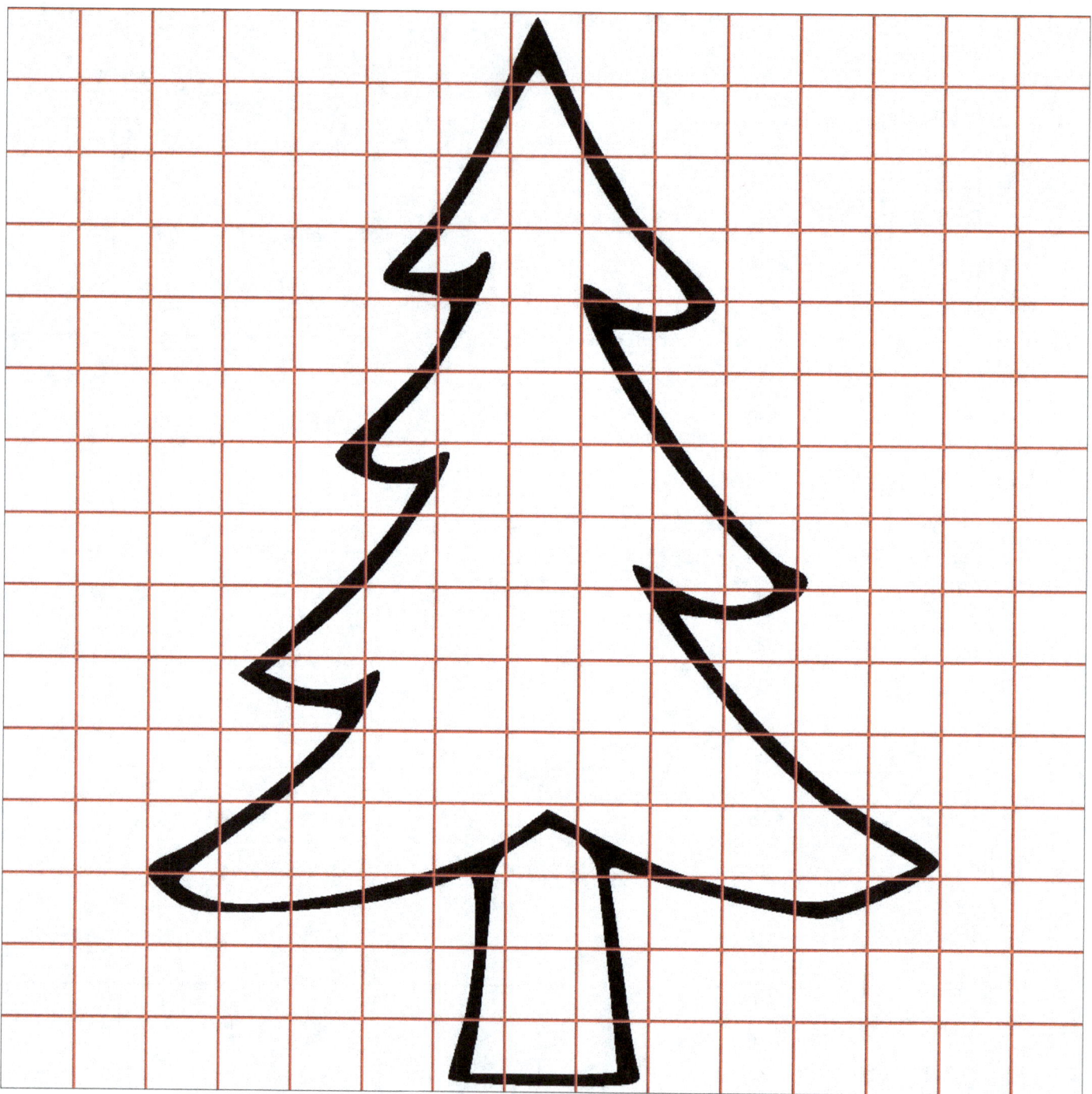

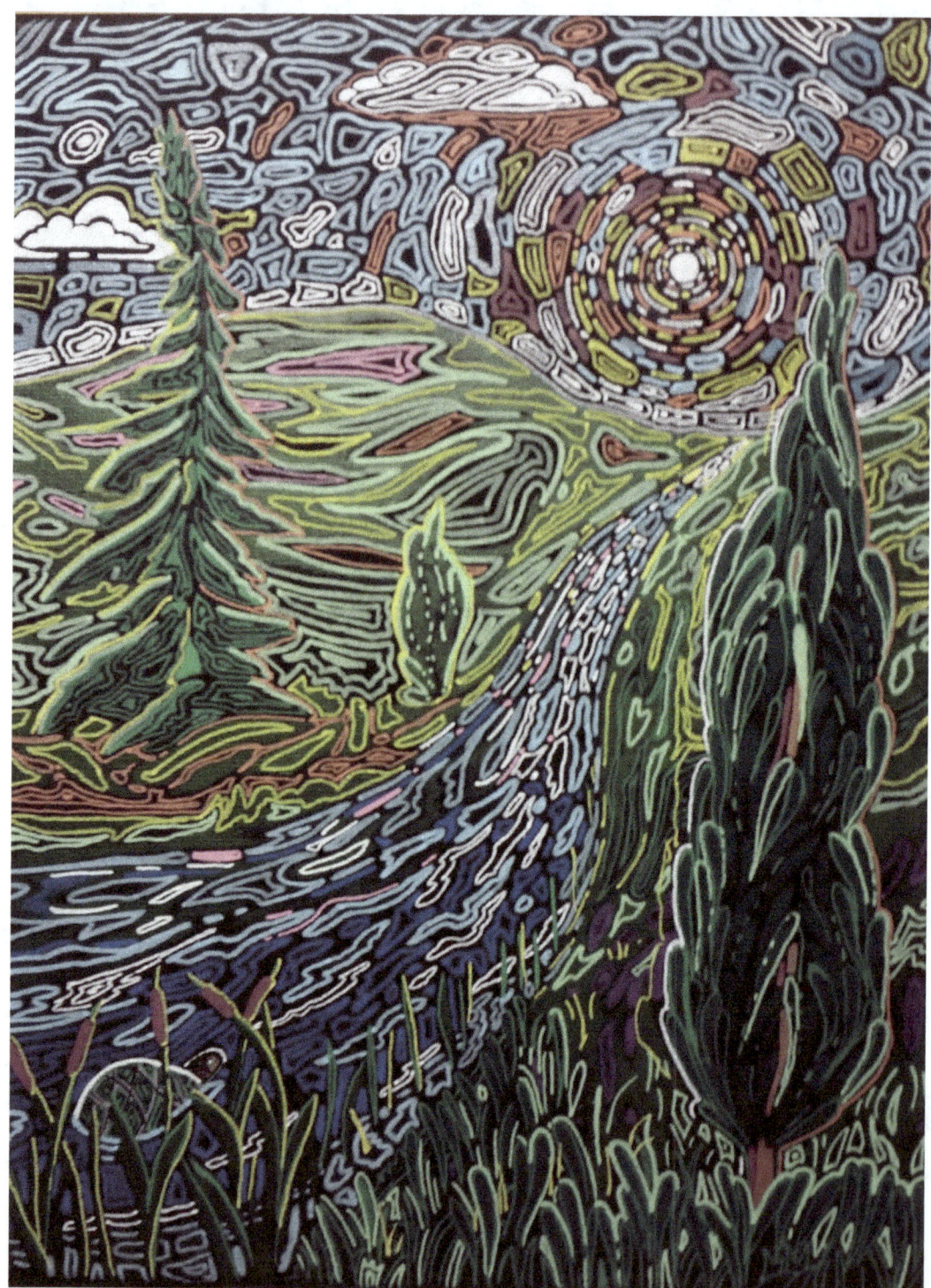

Painting by David F. Heatwole, Acrylics on canvas, 2015

I hope these last few exercises were satisfying, and you haven't thrown in the towel and thinking about giving up.

The next to last exercise with the old pine tree might be a little more fun and should be easy after all of what you completed if you completed them. This time, you'll need to use the 5 x 5 gridded-off tree from the previous page to help you finish the one halfway done on the page after that.

Once you complete that, it will be time to draw the tree entirely on your own from memory. I hope this won't intimidate you but consider this last exercise a quiz before taking the final test. Completing the test isn't a pass or fail; it is simply another challenge or exercise to attempt passing. No one is going to see how you did unless you so choose to show others. After that, you will start with another tree and set of exercises.

Good luck, you got this!

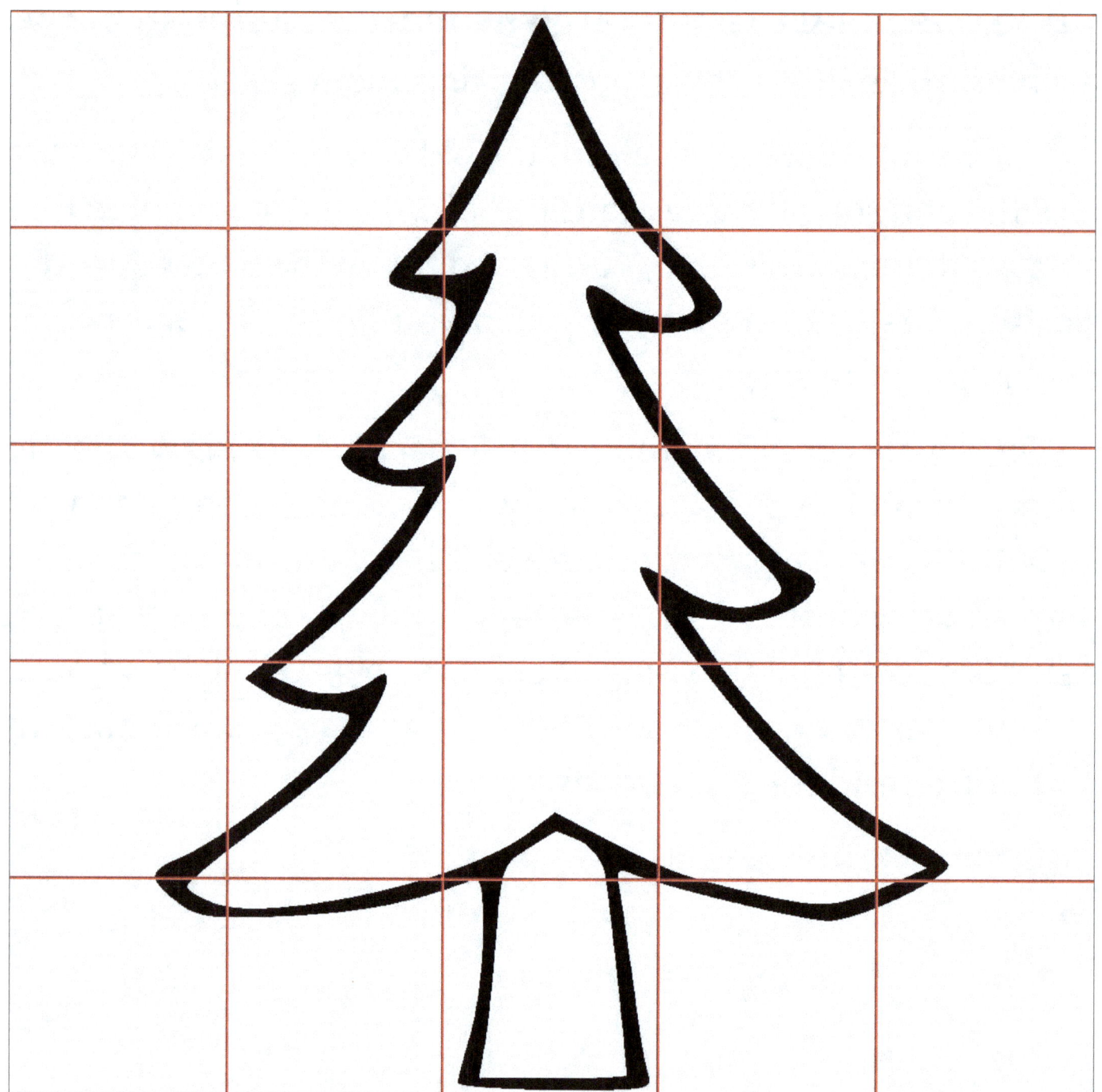

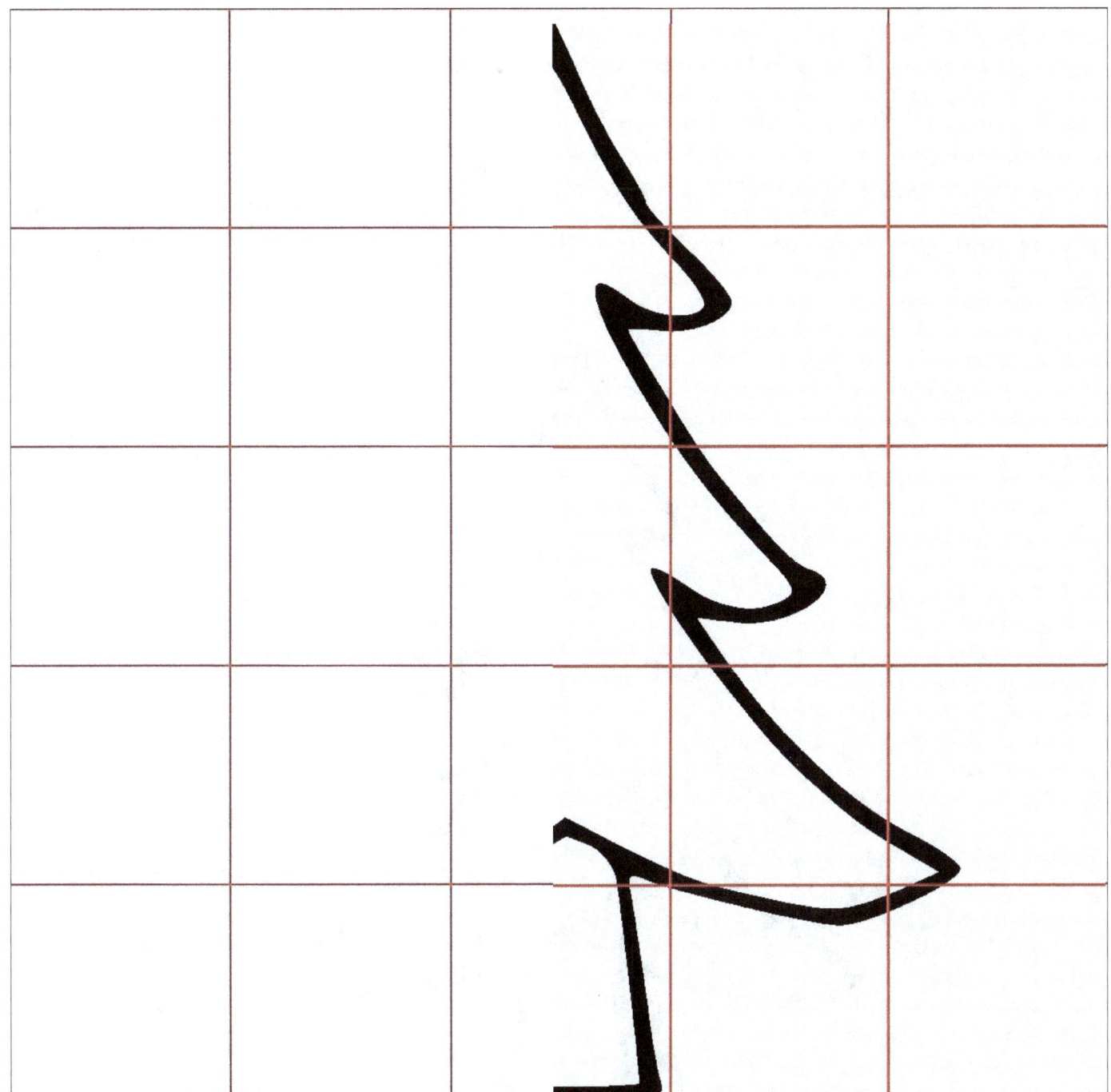

Now it is your turn to try to draw the pine tree without a grid. Use all that you learned while analyzing the tree in all the past pages. The grids should have helped you observe all the slight changes in the lines, the curves, the straight lines, the thin parts, and the thick parts of the tree. Because of all the time you've spent studying and watching, you should now be a master of this drawing.   You can do this!

DRAW IT!

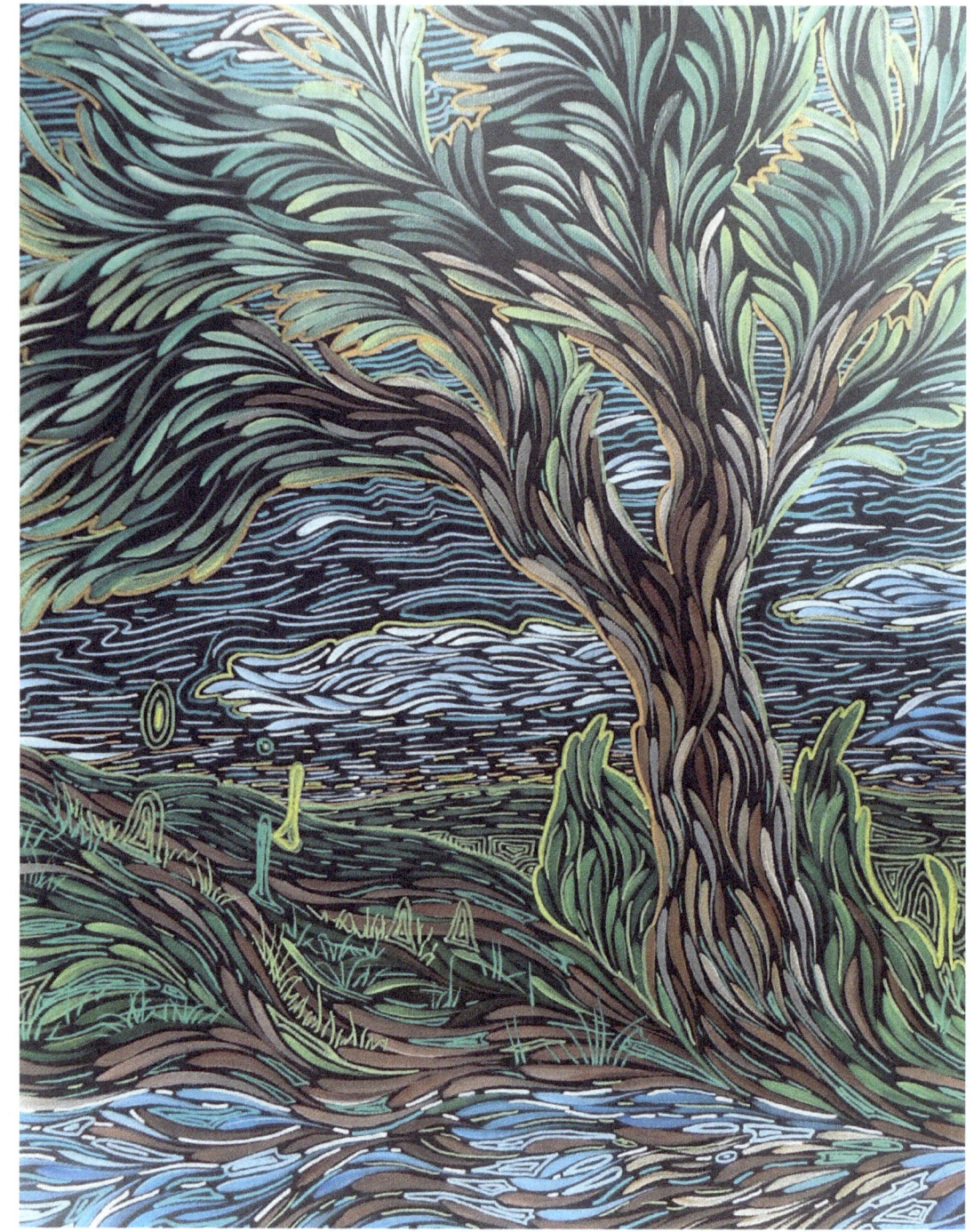

Painting by David F. Heatwole,
Acrylics on canvas, 2014

For this next tree, you might want to use a thicker black Sharpie marker; as you may know, already these markers come in various tips, the one you want to use here is called a Chisel Tip. The reason I am suggesting this is so you can create the thick line without having to draw the inner and outer parts of this thicker line like you had to do in the last exercise. TWO THINGS TO TAKE NOTE: 1.) place a piece of cardboard under the paper because the ink will probably bleed through. 2.) I created this workbook using Amazon Kindle printing services. I know, and so should you, that the paper is not premium drawing paper; THEREFORE, the ink may bleed on the paper as well. Test the marker first on a corner with a dot or a line along the border to see if it will bleed or if the line will keep its shape. Sorry about this, but I have yet to find a real publisher. Maybe if this book becomes widespread, it will be picked up by an art store or sketchbook manufacturer. Try to have fun regardless, as children have fun without significant expectations.

    This tree with a cloud-like canopy is an easy tree to draw. I contemplated having it as the first to start drawing. The only problem I noticed was that all the lines are curved and therefore not as easy to explain when discussing how to use the graph, how the lines intersect the walls of each cell, and where the lines fall within each of the individual cells. The following exercises with this tree drawing are the same as before, except this time, I have set them up in reverse, starting with a 15 x 15 graph and going up in cell size while reducing the number of cells. I have set it up to enable you to see where the curves of the leafy treetop land. It will actually get a little more challenging as you go, but you got this!

That was easy, right? The great mighty Oak reduced to only a few lines. So, you got this? Are you ready to free-draw it? Well, now is your chance. Remember this. . .when you ask any inexperienced person, regardless of age, to draw a tree, this is most likely the number one tree that every beginning artist, young and old, starts with. You, my friend, are now a step above a beginner.

DRAW IT!

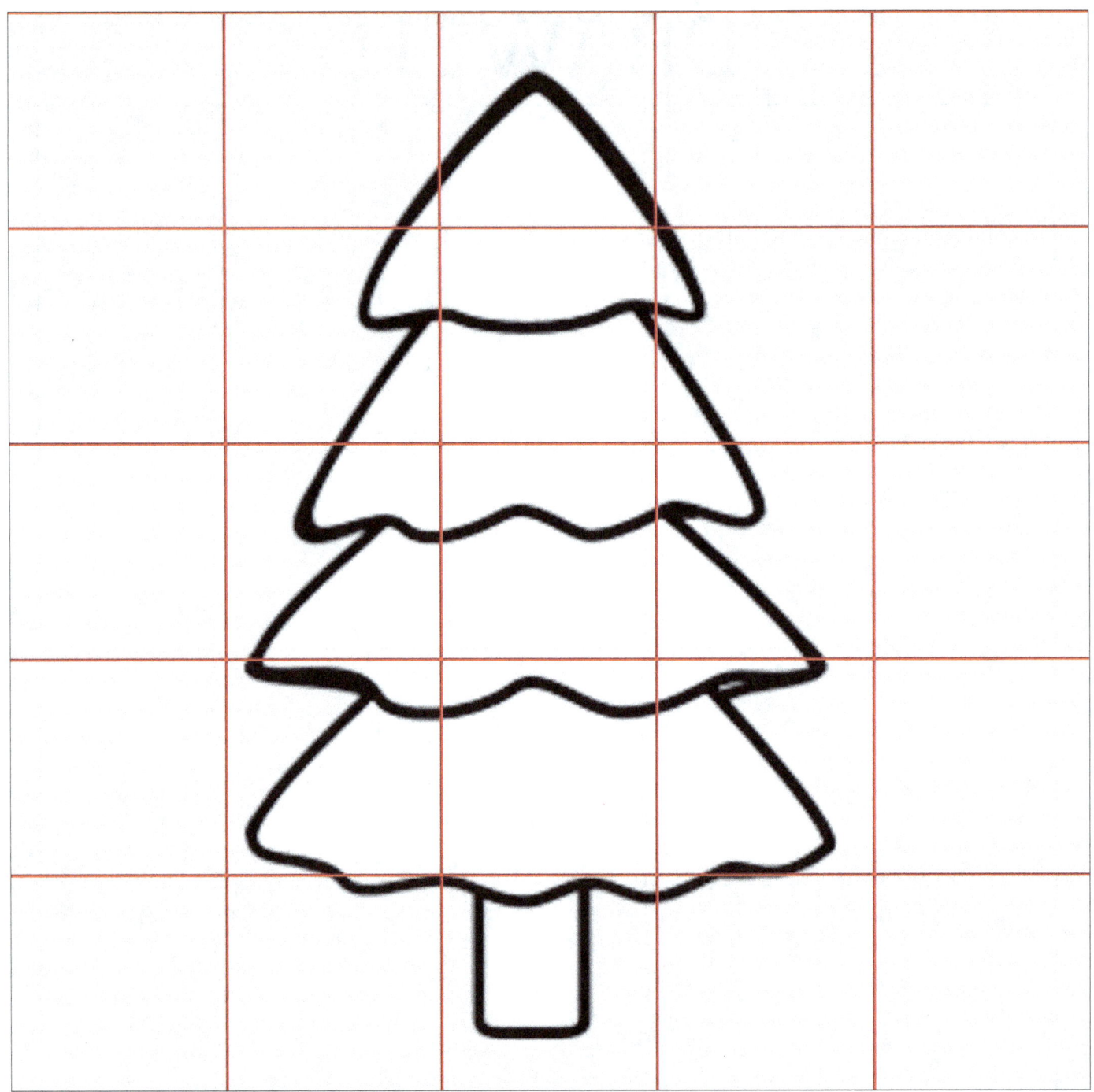

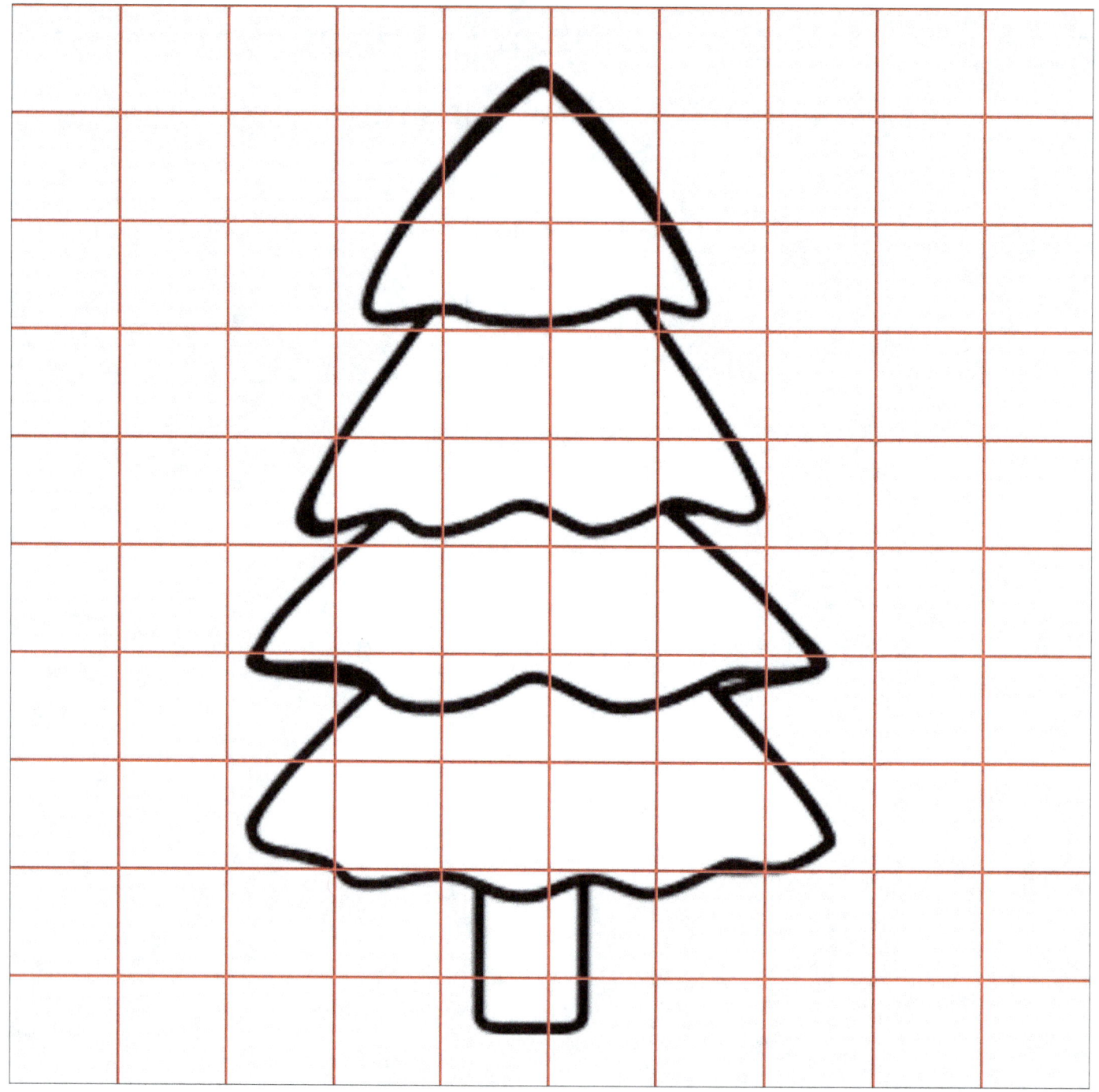

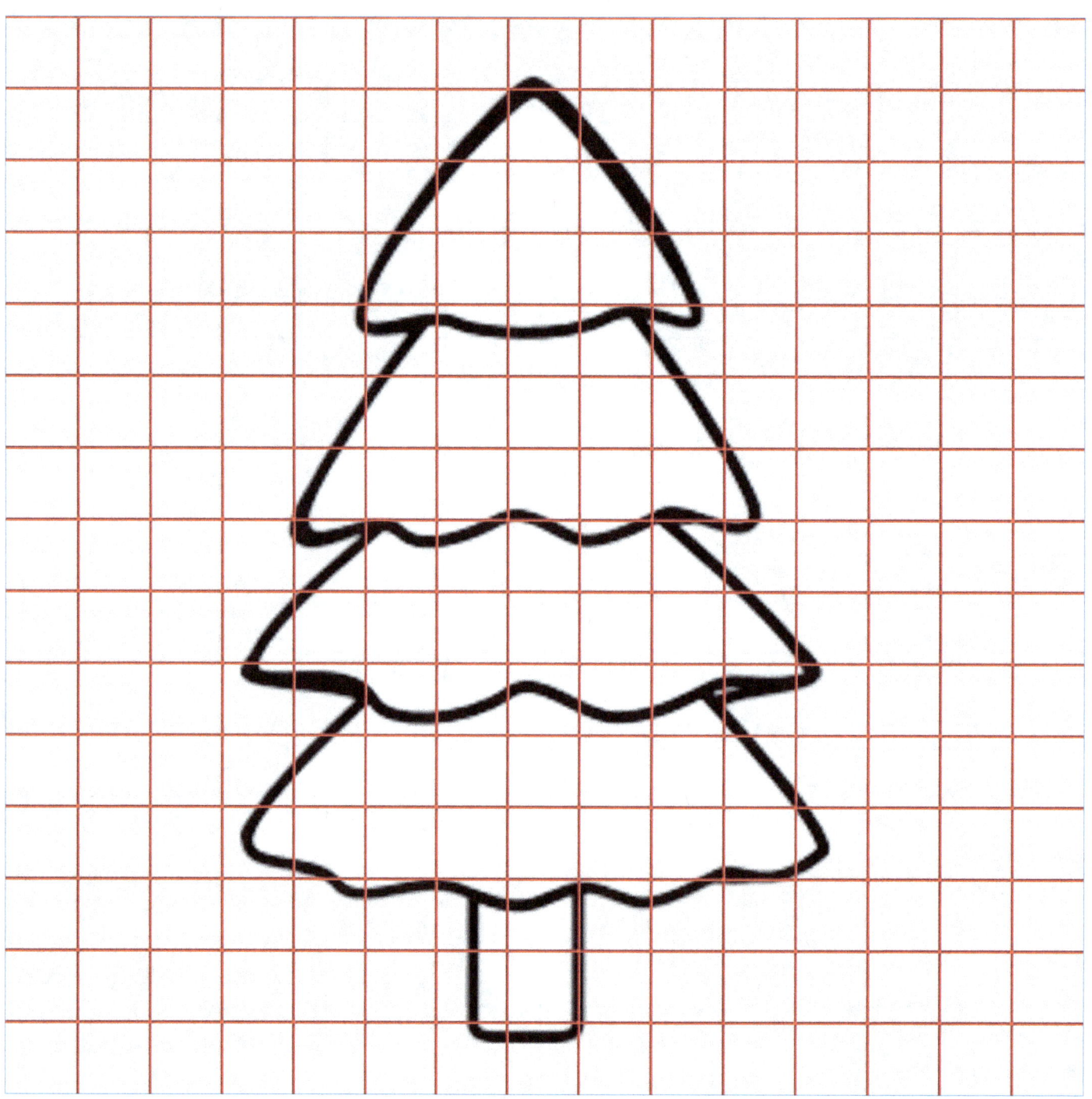

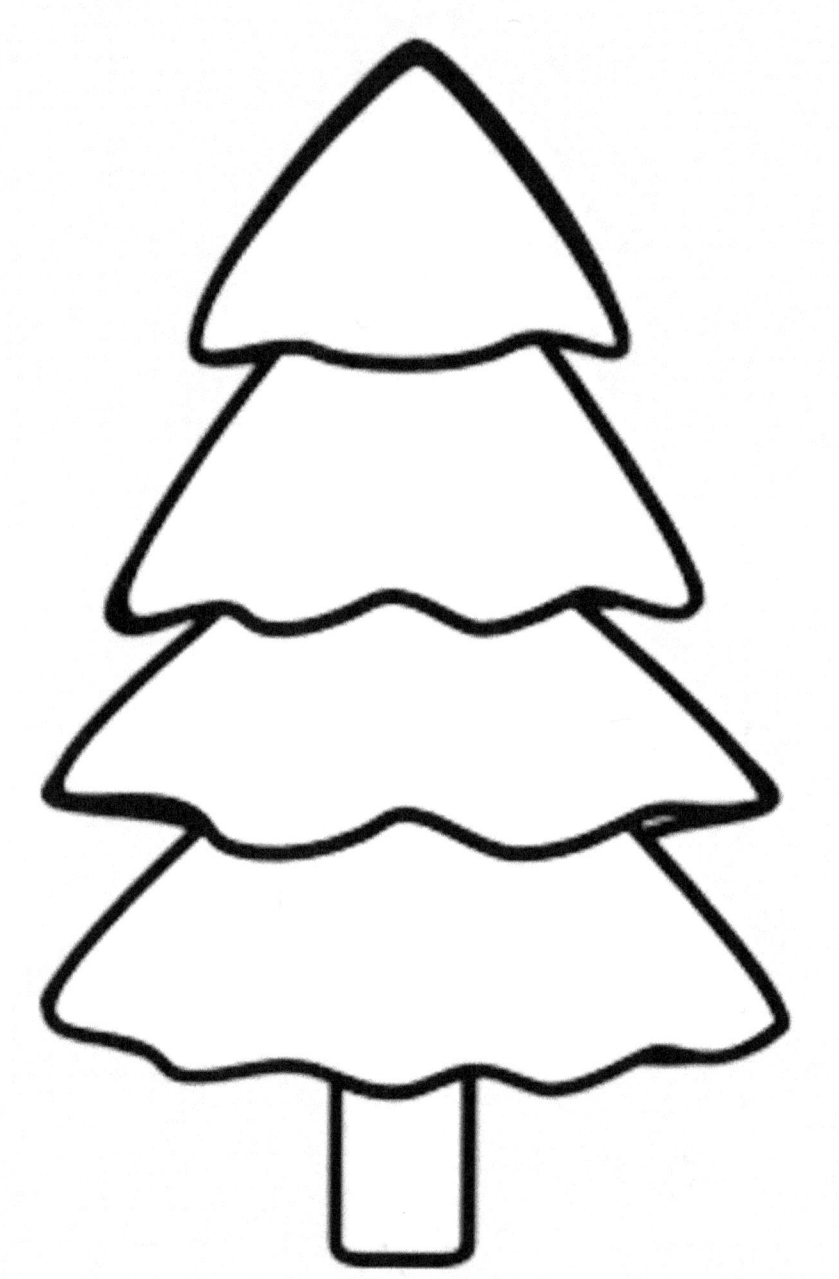

DRAW IT!

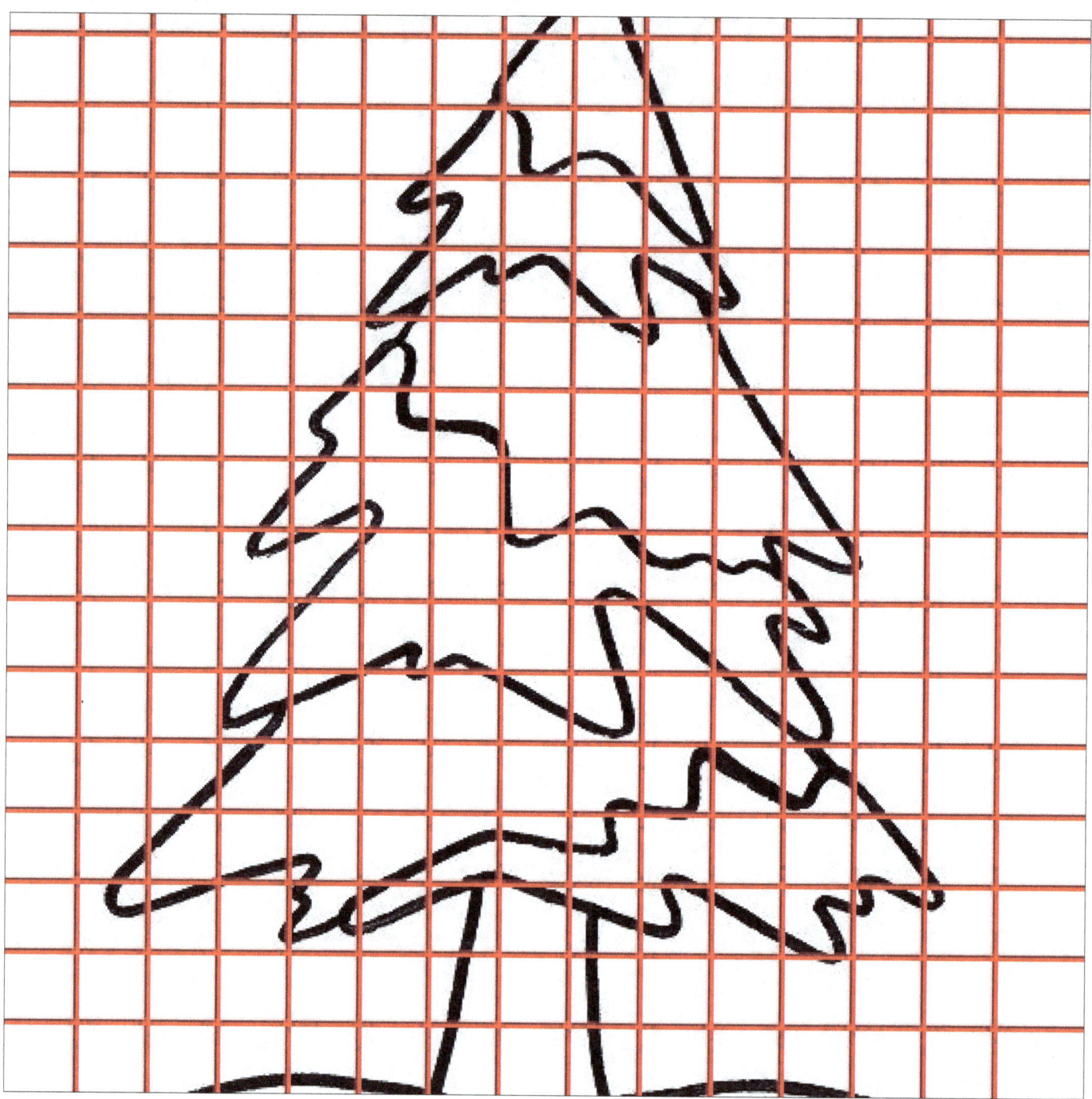

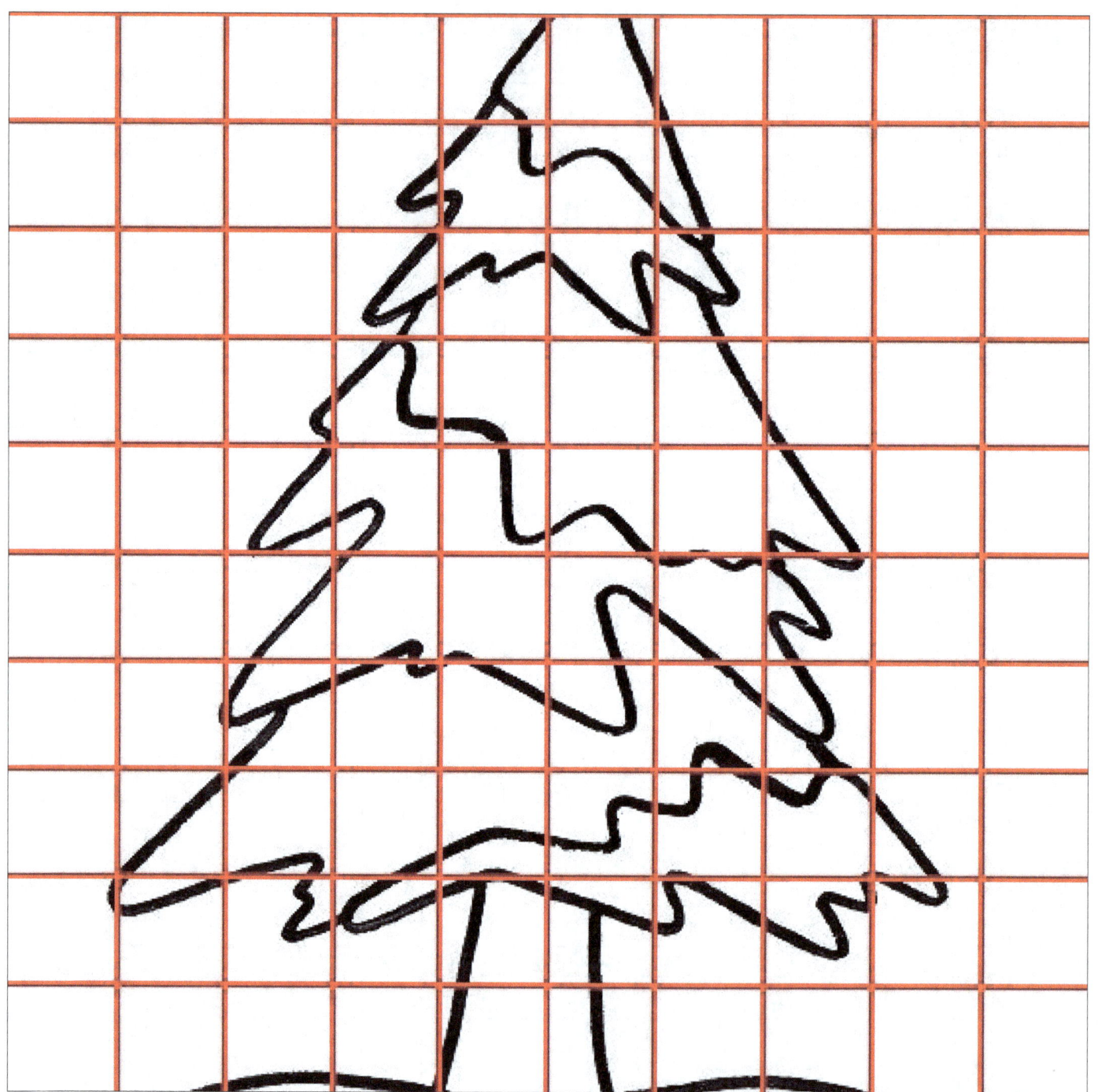

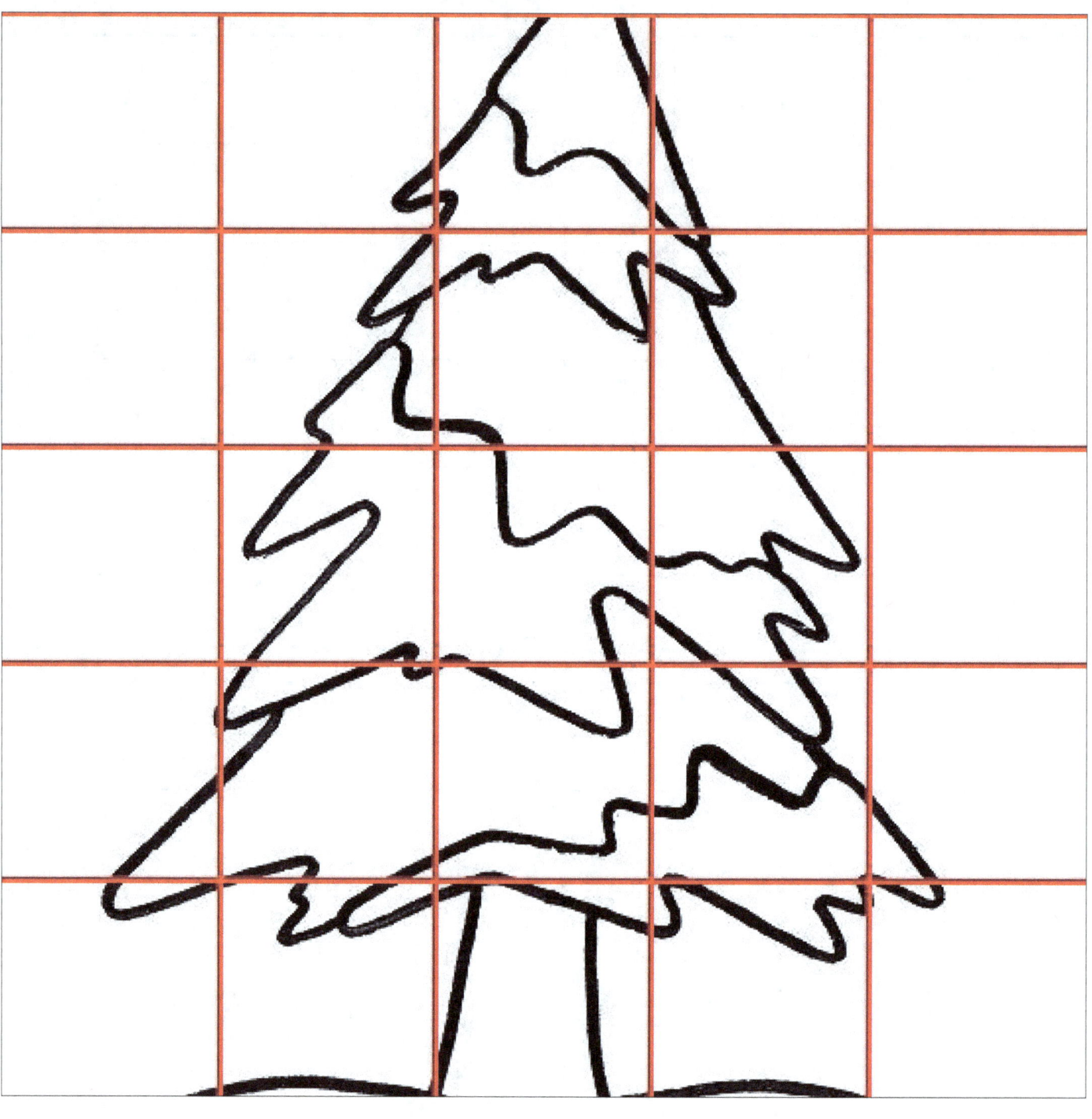

It's that time again to show yourself what you can do by looking and observing before you place your pencil on the paper. Take a deep breath, calculate where you want to start and what you have already drawn three times before getting to this final challenge. This is a more challenging tree, but you got this! It sure won't be the most difficult exercise in this book.

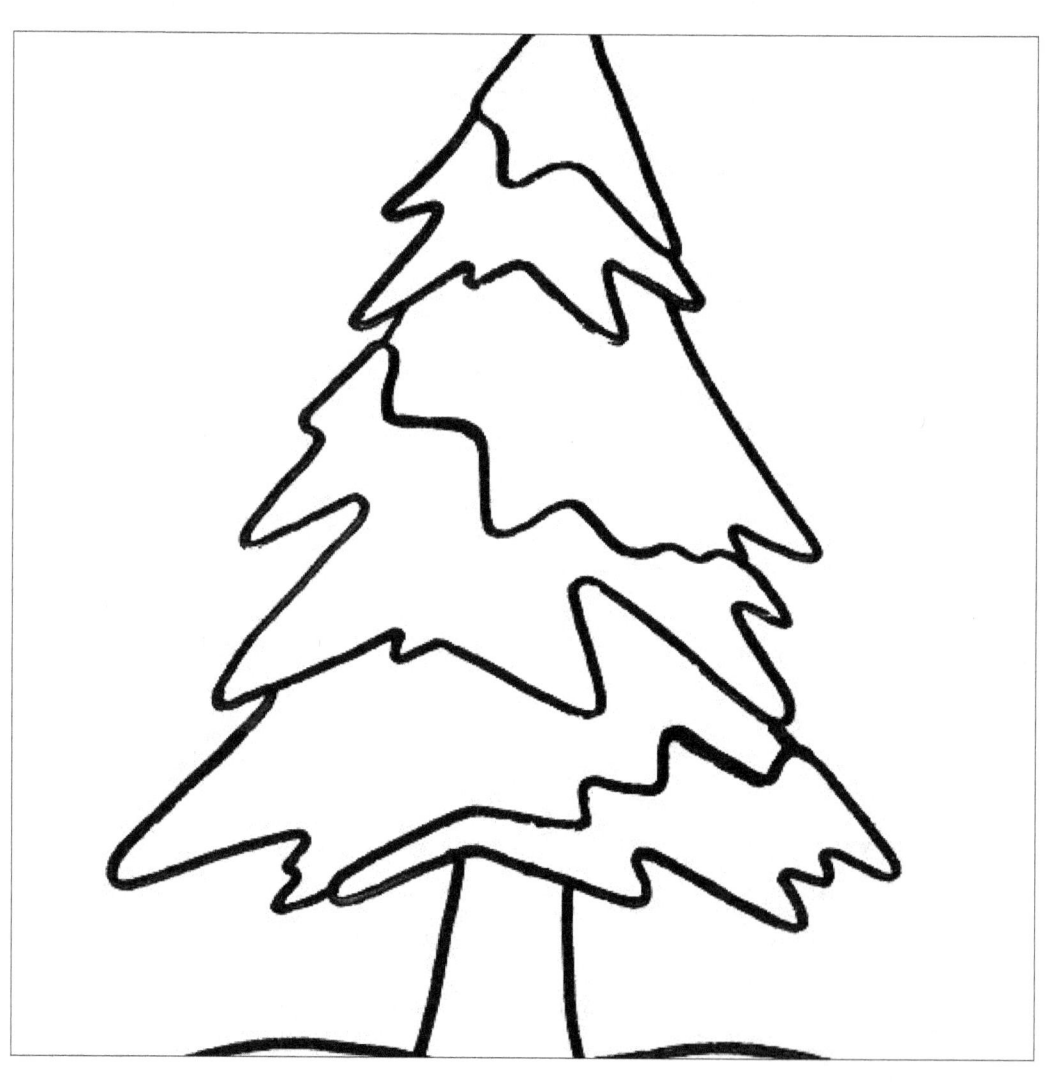

DRAW IT!

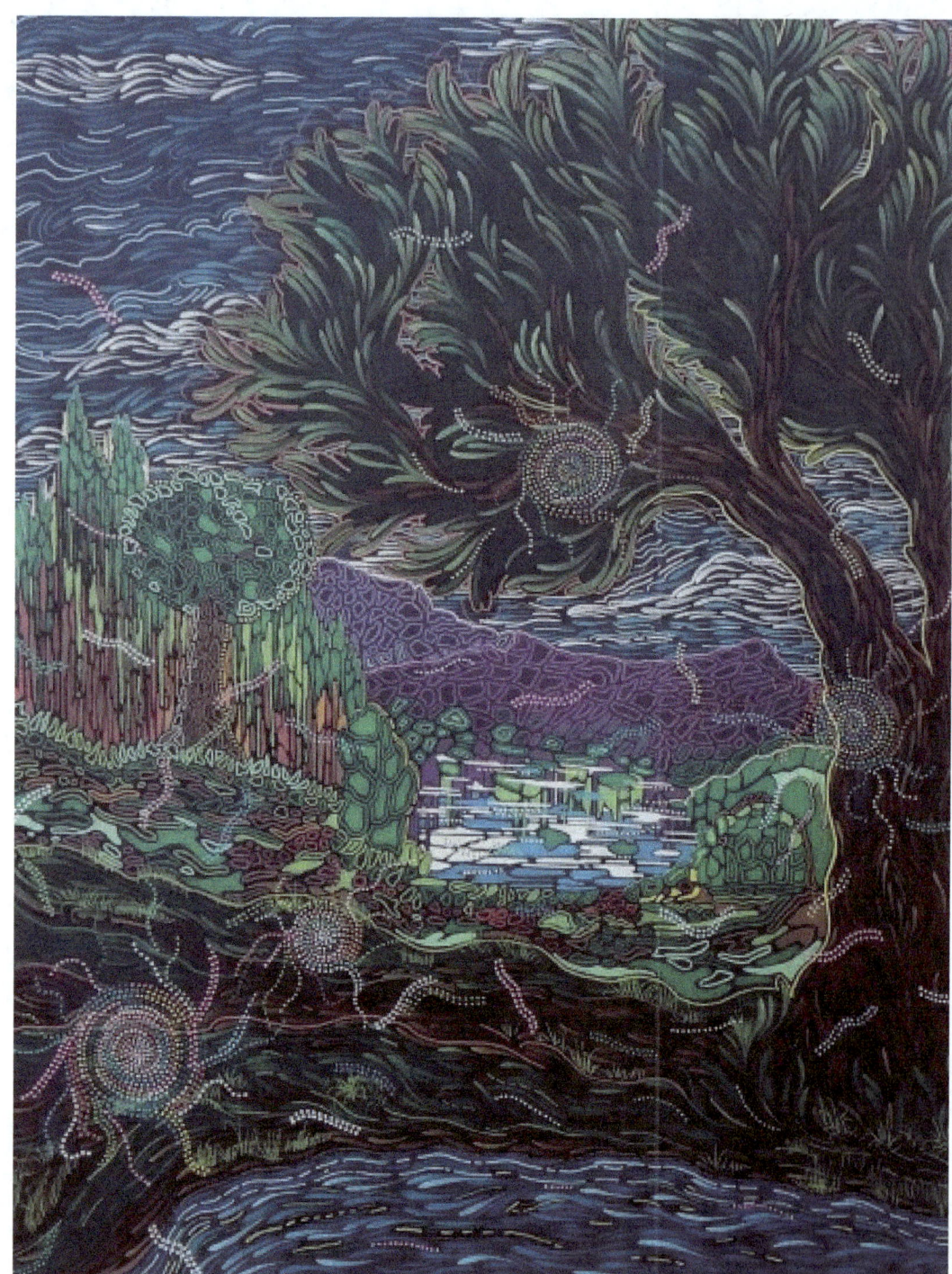

Painting by David F. Heatwole,
Acrylics on canvas, 2016

Are you ready to try some challenging tree drawings? The next tree, probably another old oak, is really nice and should be fun. It doesn't have a lot of detail, but it does have more information than the other trees you have been working with.

I believe you have had enough of the multiple graph challenges per tree drawing, and now it is time to just go for it. I have chosen for this next tree a 10 x 10 graph. You will notice that not all of the squares are exactly the same. That's okay; use the same principles when transferring the image and cut off what isn't fitting in the square grids.

After one attempt with the grid paper, it will be time to jump in and draw it freehand without the use of the grid paper.

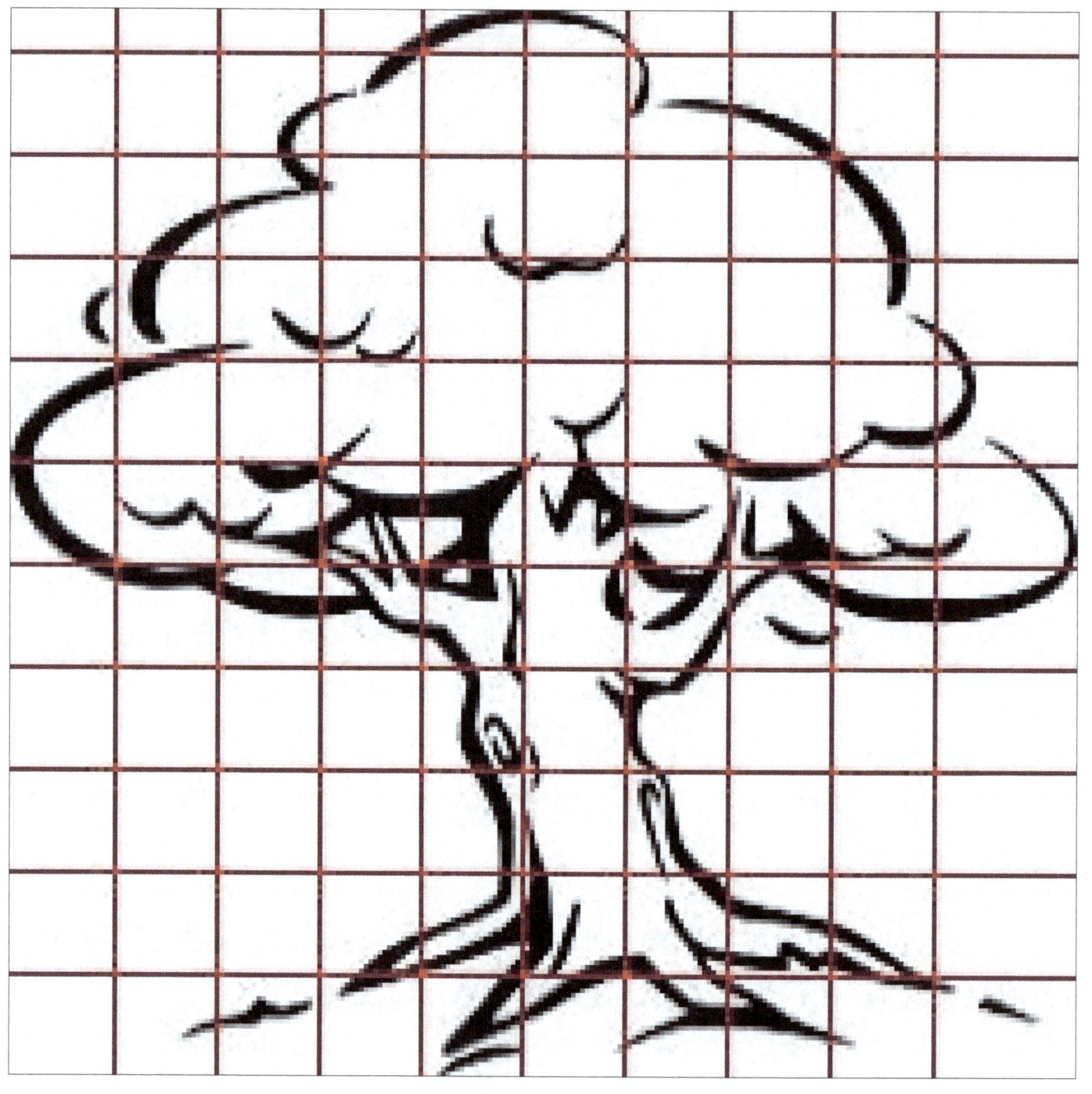

For this transfer from the gridded drawing to the grid, I have reduced its size, as you can see on the bottom right. I did this to show that the information is still the same regardless of how large or small the gridded drawing is. The grid still correlates with the larger-sized grid on the opposite page, but each cell's information is the same regardless of how I presented it on the page.

I could go as small as this...

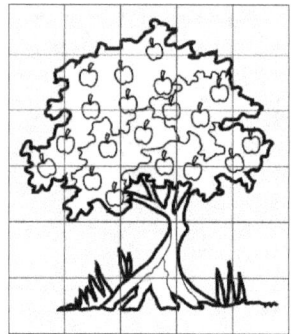

...If I wanted to make it much more difficult for you.

YOU'VE GOT THIS!!!

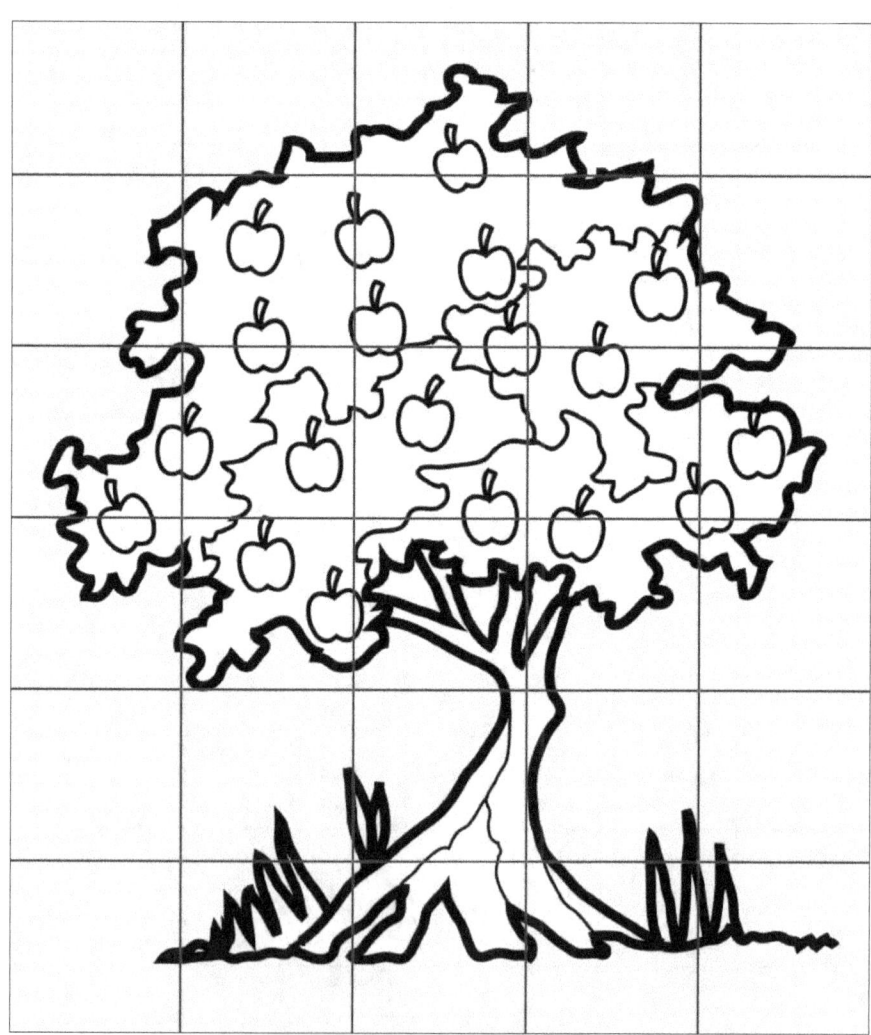

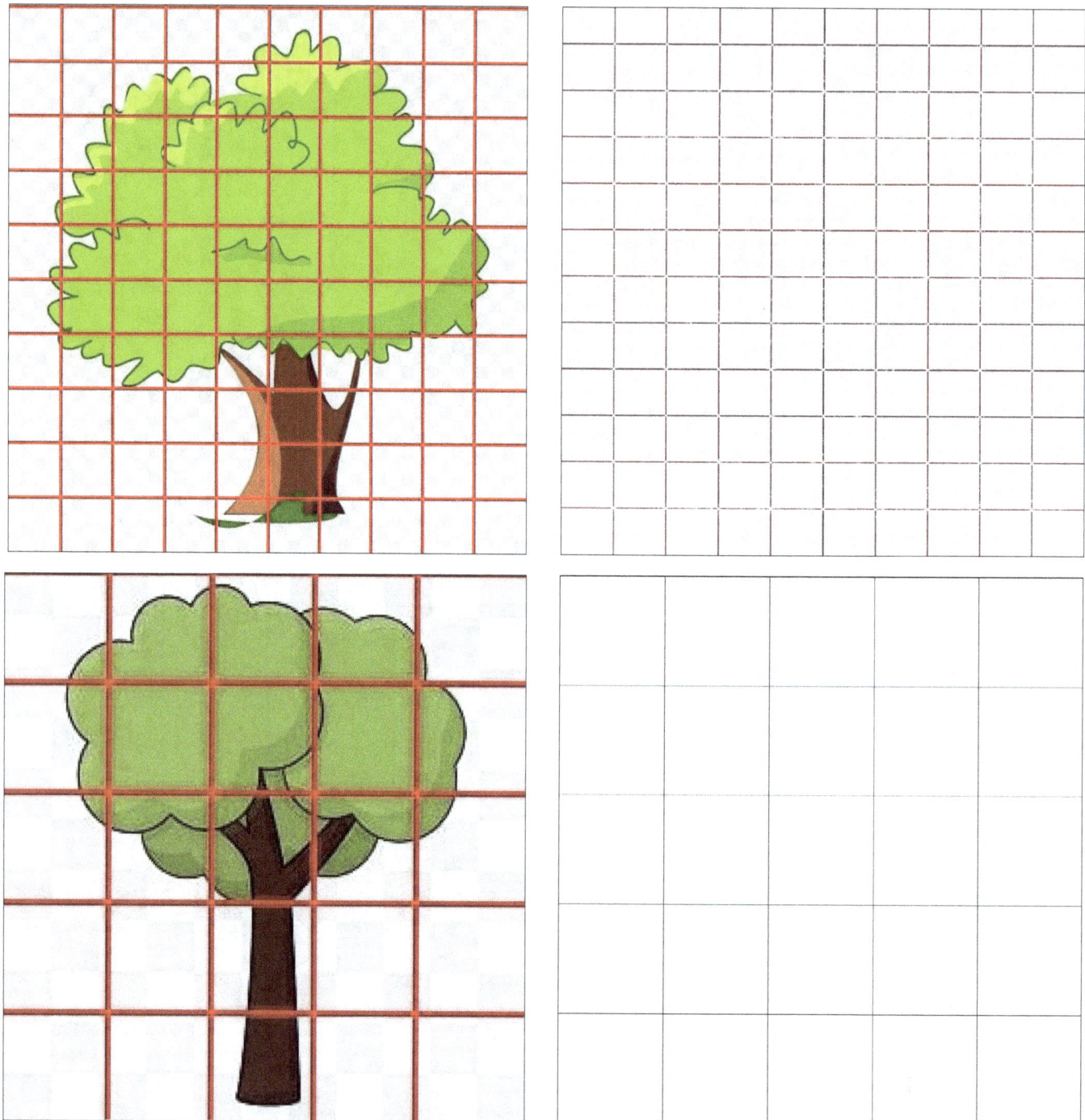

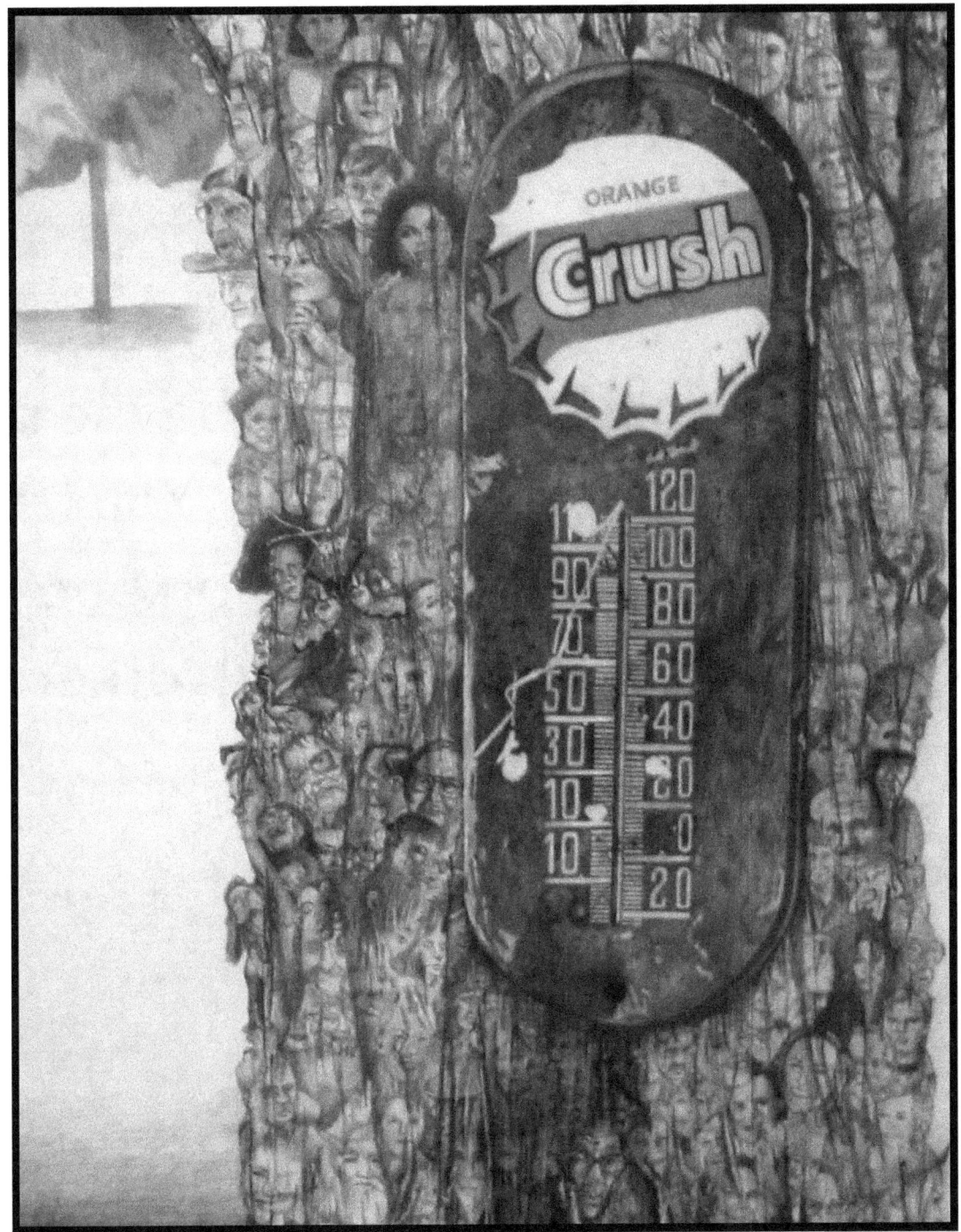

Limited Edition Print   SMILES, FROWNS & CRUSHED DREAMS   David Heatwole

HERE WE GO! This next one will be the most complicated of the line drawings. You have one chance to do it here in the workbook, but feel free to do it on your own with other paper.

You are in the home stretch! After you complete this drawing you will then have a real difficult drawing to do but I am sure you are up for the challenge – RIGHT!?!

You are about to graduate "Grid and Draw kindergarten." Take your time on these next two projects.

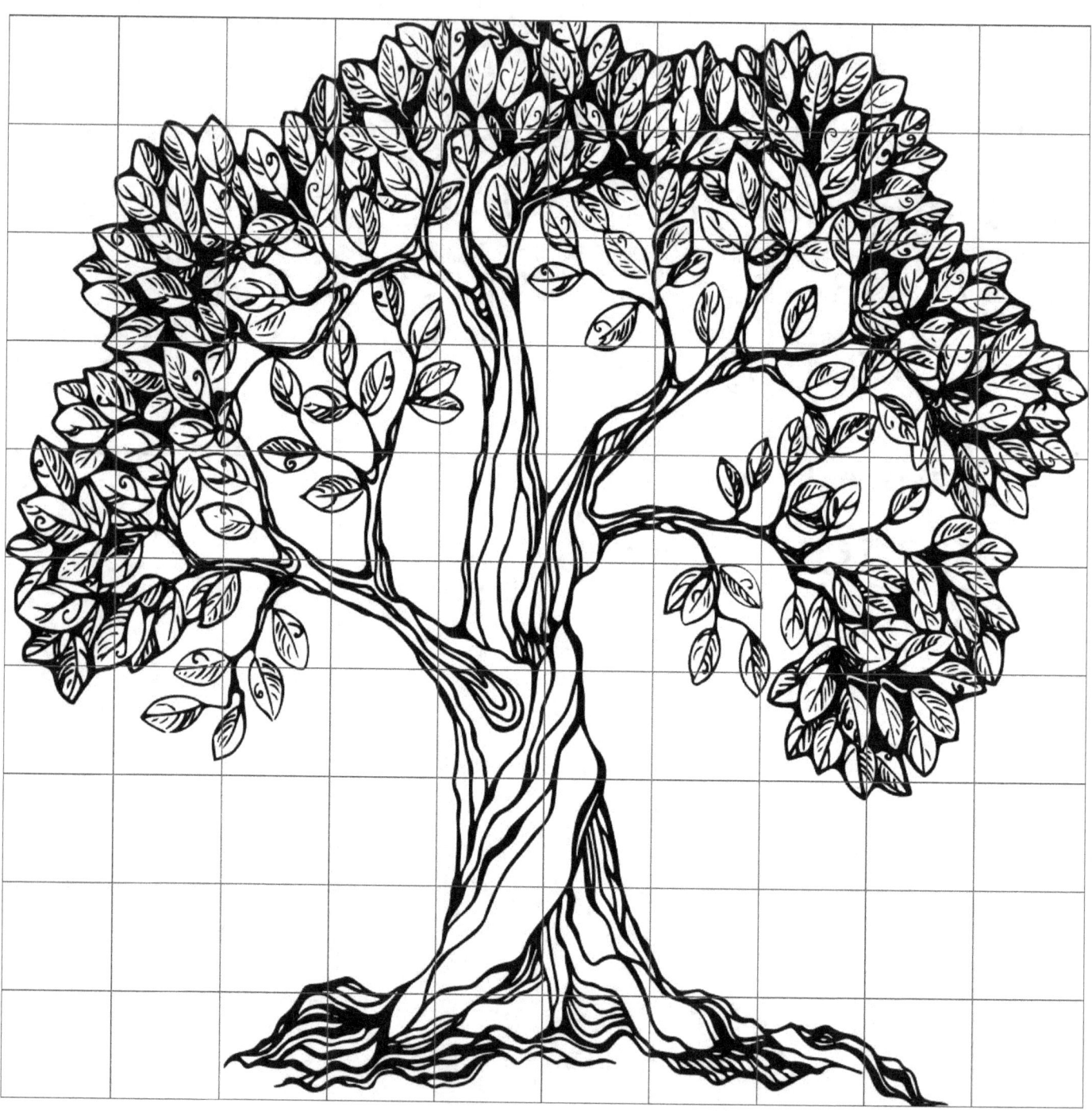

It's that time again to show yourself what you can do by looking and observing before you place your pencil on the paper. Take a deep breath, calculate where you want to start and what you have already drawn three times before getting to this final challenge. This is a more challenging tree, but you got this! It sure won't be the most difficult exercise in this book.

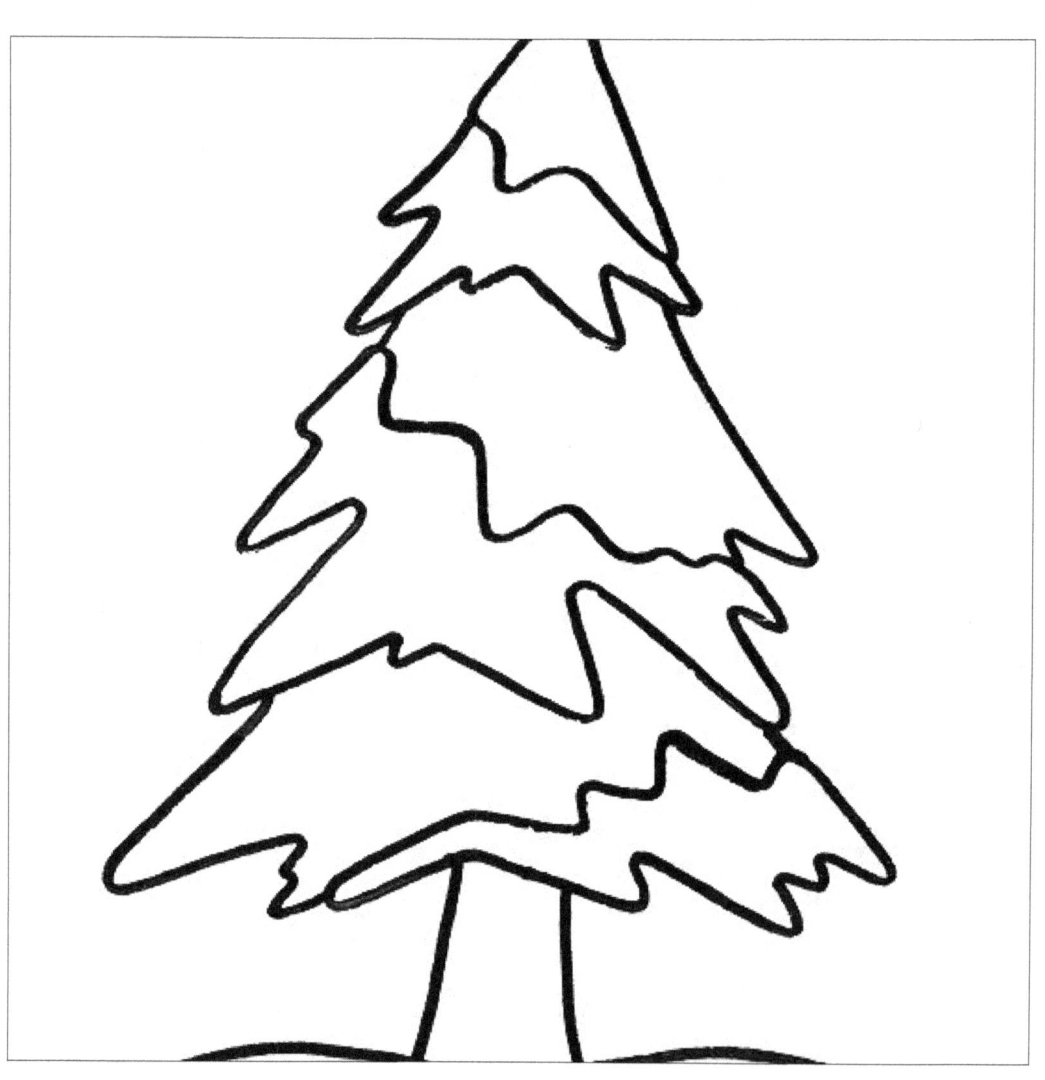

Painting by David F. Heatwole, Acrylics on canvas, 2015

NOW IS THE TIME!!! Here is a real challenge. Do the best you can and remember all you are doing is collecting and transferring information.

For this exercise, I have laid a grid on top of a photo by photographer Alex Grodkiewicz. Your job, of course, is to draw it with help from the 20 x 20 grid*. You don't have to involve color unless you so desire. Just do your best observing and copying what you see.

*I really hope the red lines overlaying the photo show up well enough. Please forgive me if they don't. Again, because I am self-publishing via Kindle, it might not be quite as perfect as I would like...OR MAYBE IT WILL BE!

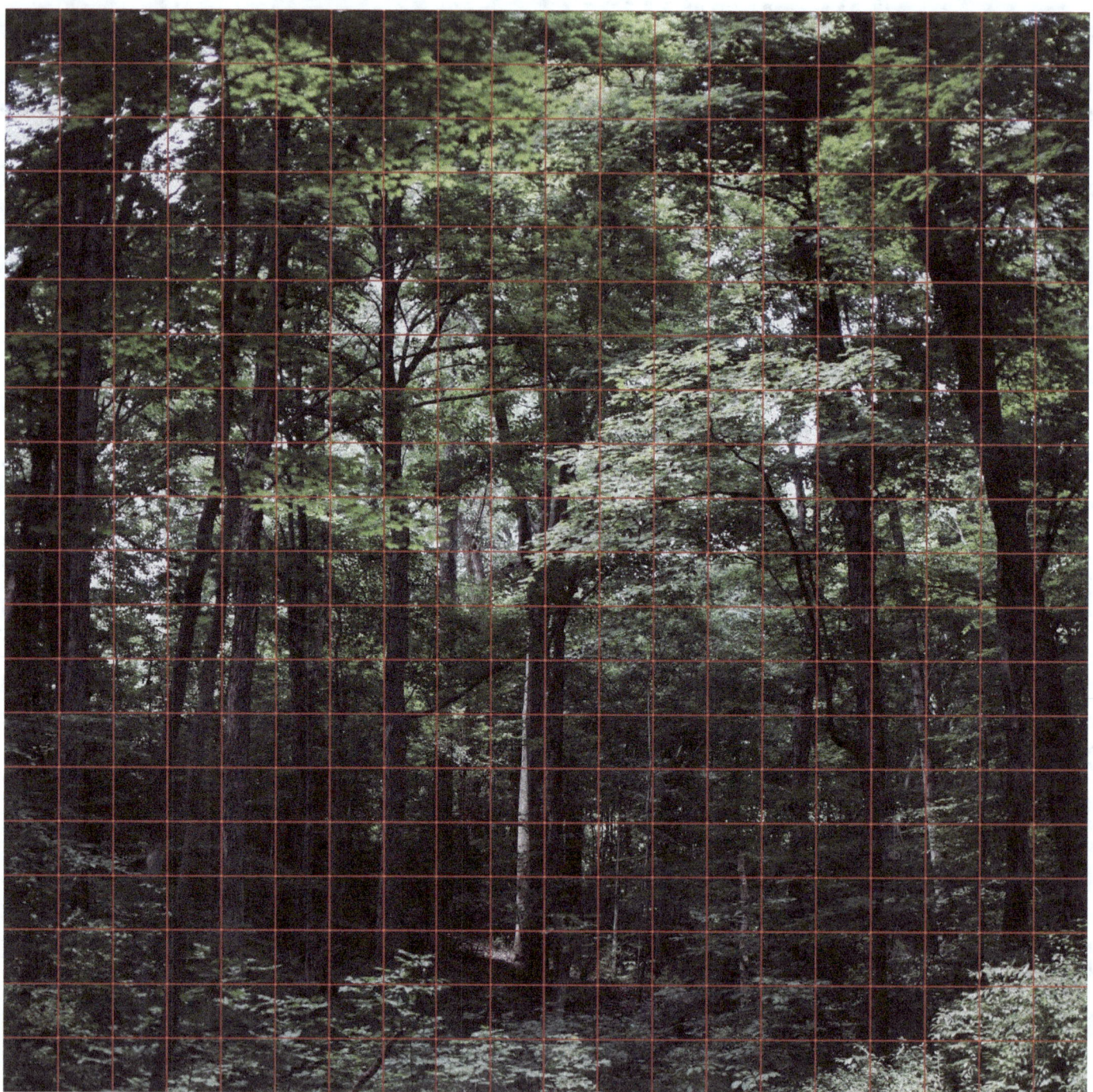

This is the last and final exercise.

I hope what I have laid out here has inspired you and helped you to grasp how a grid, regardless of the size and number of cells, can help you see what you want to draw by breaking it down into bite-sized morsels. It should also have helped you see how a grid can be used to transfer and enlarge an image to another gridded surface, be it a flat surface or a 3-D surface like a soda can. Completing these exercises should have given you a better understanding of how to patiently observe something in order to draw it. Drawing is very much like putting together a complicated puzzle but in my opinion more fun.

The photo below that you are to enlarge on the following page is simply a detail of the same image by Mr. Grodkiewicz that you copied in the last exercise.

While working on this last exercise consider giving thanks to all the people that gave us the paper we use for this book and that we use for everything under the sun.

God bless all those who have manufactured the trees and gave us paper, wood around pencils, and so much more.

BTW as I work on adding the final touches, it is Earth Day 2021.

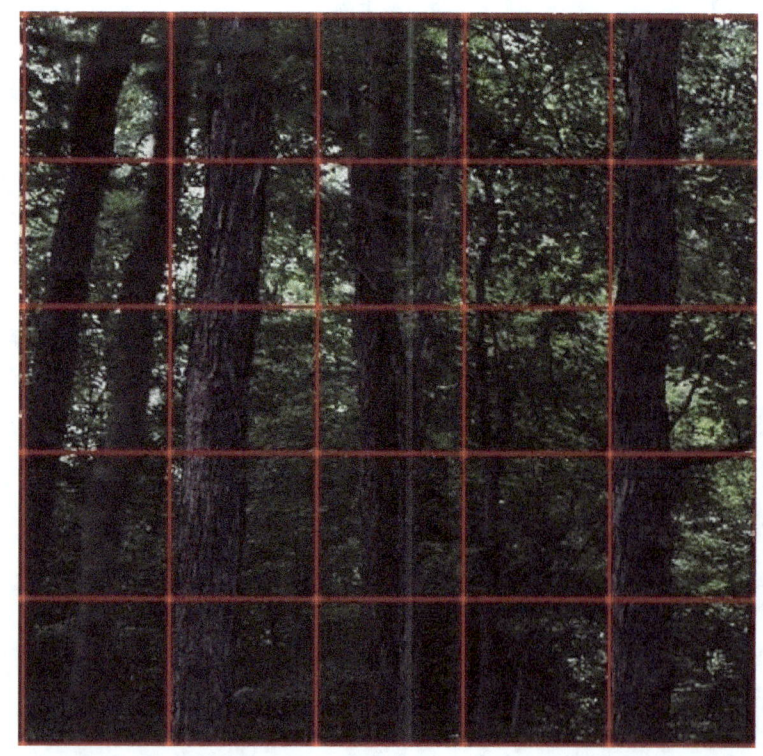

And this is where I can say, "THE END!" but I suspect it really could be "THE BEGINNING." If you took the time to really complete this workbook, you are most likely ready to continue to another stage in your art-making "hobby." Why you want to do so is beyond me; maybe it is for fun, or perhaps it is for some form of therapy. Regardless I hope it does bring you lots of joy and comfort. It won't always be easy, and sometimes it might not even be fun. Ultimately though, I hope that it will help you contemplate life and all the Who, What, Where, Why, and How questions that have plagued humankind since our first conception.

Most importantly, if you don't have the answer already, I hope you find the answer to WHO. Who made you? Who made all of this? Who loves you unconditionally? Who forgives you? It was the art-making process that helped me find him (you know who I am talking about), and I hope it helps you.

God bless you, your efforts, and your hands.

Artfully Yours,

Do it Dave

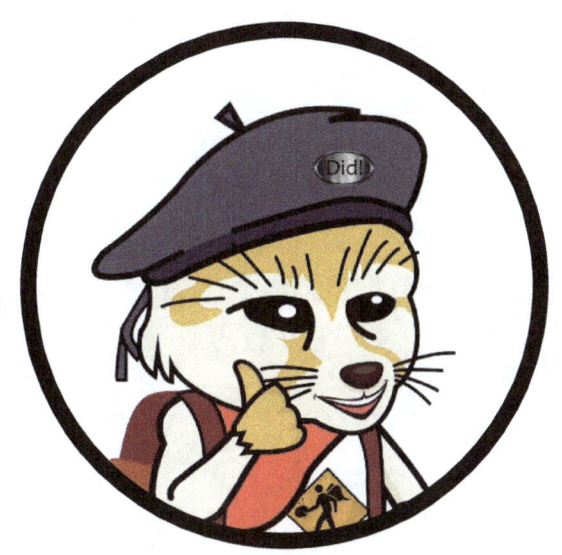

More tips and lessons coming to www.ThisArtistsDream.com

www.ingramcontent.com/pod-product-compliance
Lightning Source LLC
Chambersburg PA
CBHW062334220526
45469CB00008B/2717